My God is Real

In Search of God

Hidden Warfare

ISBN 0 85476 869 6

Published by
KINGSWAY PUBLICATIONS
Lottbridge Drove, Eastbourne, BN23 6NT, England.
Email: books@kingsway.co.uk

Designed and produced for the publishers by
Bookprint Creative Services, P. O. Box 827, BN21 3YJ, England.
Printed in Great Britain.

Reproduced from the original typesetting
of the single-volume editions.

My God is Real

DAVID WATSON

KINGSWAY PUBLICATIONS
EASTBOURNE

THIS BOOK
IS DEDICATED TO ANNE

Contents

Introduction

A desire for reality is almost universal. If at the moment there is a revolt against the established Christian Church, it is in part a healthy distaste for all that is hollow and humbug. 'Somehow God has become for most people, and even for many practising Christians, unreal', writes Bernadine Bishop. 'The God we want must be real. He must be a convincing personal experience. The God who is not real to me, revealing and operating all that is deepest and most personal in my being, is no God to me' (*The God I want*). Fair enough! The question is: how can God become real, if indeed he exists at all?

This is a question which many have asked. 'My soul thirsts for God, for the living God', cried the psalmist (Psalm 42:2). 'Oh, that I knew where I might find him', complained Job (Job 23:3). 'I sought him, but found him not; I called him, but he gave no answer', recounts the bride in the Song of Solomon (Song 3:1). Michel Quoist expresses the feelings of many:

> *Lord, do you hear me? . . .*
> *Lord, I can no longer find my own door.*
> *I grope around blindly,*
> *I knock against my own walls, my own boundaries.*
> *I hurt myself,*
> *I am in pain . . .*
> *Lord, Lord, do you hear me?*
> *Lord, show me my door,*
> *   take me by the hand.*
> *Open the door,*
> *Show me the way,*
> *The path leading to joy, to light.*
> *But, Lord, do you hear me?*
>   *Prayers of Life* Logos Books

Why is this search for the reality of God so important?

First, there is today a general restlessness. If there is disillusionment concerning conventional established

Christianity, there is also dissatisfaction with what is apparently the only alternative, Colin Wilson, a confessed rebel against the Establishment, states that he is still searching for a 'perfect freedom': 'We need a new religion to unite us and give us purpose ... my deepest interest is religion. My deepest need – to create my own.' In other words he, together with the great majority, is searching for reality. We see this restlessness expressed in pop songs and modern films, whether by the Beatles or Bergman.

According to Pascal there is a conflict between reason and the passions. If only man had 'reason without passions ... if he had only passions without reason ... but having both, he cannot be without strife, being unable to be at peace with the one without being at war with the other' (*Penseés* No. 412). The conflict is revealed in sexual licence, experiments with drugs, and the persistent search for an 'ultimate' experience. All this is simply an attempt to discover the true meaning of life.

Secondly, in the minds of a great many people, there is a distorted image of the Christian faith. When my father died I was going through some family papers and possessions, and I came across an old painting of one of my ancestors. It looked rather dusty, and in my impatience I wanted to throw it into the dustbin, where it seemed to belong. As far as I was concerned it was a useless relic of bygone days. Many have the same impatience with Christianity: 'a useless relic of bygone days'. However, I did not throw the picture into the dustbin, and today I am very glad. It was found to be an extremely valuable painting, and suddenly this dreary dusty ancestral portrait acquired a new respect from the members of our family! And I would suggest that if, at the moment, many are tempted to reject the Christian faith as a useless relic, they may be in for a great surprise.

Christ himself said that the Christian life could be thought of as treasure discovered in a field, or a pearl of great price. Therefore the heart of the Christian faith is something precious and of great value. The person who thinks that Christ wants to turn his life into a musty old attic filled with outdated ideas has not begun to understand the true meaning of being a Christian. Christ said:

'I have come that men may have life, and may have it in all its fullness' (John 10:10 NEB).

Thirdly, Christ said some startling things about himself and our relationship with him. We shall be looking at some of these more fully in the rest of this book; but in the Sermon on the mount he said:

Not everyone who calls me 'Lord, Lord' will enter the kingdom of Heaven, but only those who do the will of my heavenly Father. When that day comes, many will say to me, 'Lord, Lord, did we not prophesy in your name, cast out devils in your name, and in your name perform many miracles?' Then I will tell them to their face, 'I never knew you: out of my sight, you and your wicked ways!'

Matthew 7:21–23 NEB

According to Jesus Christ, we shall all one day have to give an account of our lives; and on that day, the Day of Judgment, the crucial question will be 'What place has Christ had in your life?'

If the things Christ said are not true, then the sooner we throw this Christianity into a funeral pyre the better. Many down the centuries, have tried to do so, and many would like to do it today. If Christ's words are not true, our churches can become bingo halls, the Bible can go into a museum, ministers and missionaries can stop wasting their time; and thousands of Christians throughout the world can stop being persecuted for the sake of their Master.

On the other hand, if Christ's teaching is the truth, the position is very different. There may need to be radical changes in our lives, a new life altogether. What is necessary is that we should know what real Christianity is all about: and that is the purpose of this book.

One final point of introduction. God never promises to reveal himself purely to satisfy our intellectual curiosity. There is one essential condition, and that is honesty. The person who is determined to justify his unbelief will never discover that God is real. But to the one who is honest in his search, honest about his doubts and confusion, honest about his intellectual problems, and honest enough to examine the evidence with as fresh and open a mind as he can bring to it, God will make himself known.

I found this to be true in my own experience when I went up to university as a professing humanist. I had never found the reality of God in my own life, and therefore tried to convince myself that he simply did not exist. However, with the help of a friend, I looked at the Christian faith again, acted on the evidence I could see, and since that time have not doubted that *My God is real*.

CHAPTER ONE

The man who is God

We must start at the right place; and the right place in our search for the reality of God is the person of Jesus Christ. Dr Griffith Thomas once wrote: 'Christianity is the only religion in the world which rests on the person of its founder' (*Christianity is Christ* Longmans, 1925).

Some may think that this is the wrong starting-point. They would say that it is pointless to try to prove that Christ is the *Son* of God when they cannot believe in God's existence in the first place. 'Prove God's existence first,' they would say, 'then we will consider our attitude to Christ.'

However, our reason for starting at Christ is important. What do men know about God, from their own natural wisdom? Virtually nothing. As soon as man begins to seek for God he is baffled and confused, groping in the dark, out of his depth. Nor should it surprise us that he feels lost in his search for God, because if God exists he is infinite, and man is finite. How could a finite being possibly comprehend infinity? Paul said that man by wisdom cannot know God and cannot find God; God is altogether beyond his reach. We should all be incurably agnostic if God had not revealed himself. But the Christian contention is that God *has* revealed himself: through the Old Testament prophets, through the Jewish nation, through the Scriptures, but supremely in the person of Jesus Christ; and Christ is therefore rightly our starting-point.

Most people would agree that Christ was at least a good religious teacher. I have never yet met anyone who has seriously questioned this, though many would add that he was nothing more. All too often people are quick to dismiss the Christian faith because of some inconsistency they can see in the professing Christian world round them, but very seldom are such critics thorough in their examination of the person of Christ himself.

Who is Jesus Christ? This question is often asked in the Gospels. On one occasion he calmed a storm on the Sea of Galilee, and his disciples asked: 'What sort of man is this?' (Matthew 8:27). On another, he made some devastating claims about himself, and his opponents asked, 'Who on earth do you think you are?' Christ himself asked, 'Who do men say that I am?' (Mark 8:27).

The disciples were convinced of the divinity of Christ, not by theological argument, but by personal experience over the greater part of three years. We know, said John, because 'we have heard, ... we have seen with our eyes ... and touched with our hands' (1 John 1:1). What evidence brought them to this unshakable conclusion?

HIS CLAIMS

We are not limited to stories of his power as it was demonstrated two thousand years ago. He is still revealing himself in astonishing ways in the lives of people today; but for the moment I want to concentrate primarily on the New Testament.

INDIRECT CLAIMS
His miracles

The evidence for his divinity does not rest on these, but they were so striking that great crowds gathered round him. When a paralysed man was brought to him, he immediately said, with authority, 'Your sins are forgiven'. The Scribes (the bright theologians of the time) who were present knew perfectly well what this implied. Their cry was: 'It is blasphemy! Who can forgive sins but God alone?' And Christ, intending to drive home this very conclusion, replied 'That you may know that the Son of Man has authority on earth to forgive sins' (and then he turned to the paralysed man) 'I say to you, rise, take up your pallet and go home'. And immediately the man got up, took up his bed, and walked off. And they were all astounded (Mark 2:1–12).

Take another example. Thomas, the disciple, was filled with doubts about the divinity and resurrection of Christ. So the risen Christ came to him and said 'Put your finger

here, and see my hands; and put out your hand, and place
it in my side' (John 20:26–29). In other words, 'Touch
my scars, see for yourself!' Thomas answered, 'My Lord
and my God'. Now what did Christ do? Did he say
'Thomas, you must never call me that, I am not your
God'? Not at all. He accepted the worship of this disciple.
He allowed him to call him 'My God'. Indeed, he gently
rebuked him for his unbelief, because he had never trusted
in Christ's divinity before. If we read on to the Acts of the
Apostles, and see Paul and Barnabas healing a cripple at
Lystra, we find a striking contrast. When the miracle
occurred the crowds came out of the temple with oxen
and garlands to offer sacrifices to Paul and Barnabas,
because they believed that they must surely be gods. Paul
and Barnabas were horrified. 'Why are you doing this?
We also are men, of like nature with you, and bring you
good news, that you should turn from these vain things to
a living God' (Acts 14:8–18). Yet Christ calmly accepted
as his right the worship of his disciple.

His teaching

Two things are clear about Christ's teaching. First, it is
incredibly self-centred; secondly, if it is true, it is of
enormous importance for us today. People are hungry and
thirsty for something which satisfies; they know deep
within themselves that their lives are empty. Jesus said, 'I
am the bread of life ... if anyone eats of this bread, he will
live for ever' (John 6:35, 51). I am the Living Water; 'if
anyone thirst, let him come to me and drink' (John 7:37).
Many today are searching for God, but they do not know
where to find him, or even whether he exists. Jesus said, 'I
am the way, and the truth, and the life; no one comes to
the Father, but by me' (John 14:6). Many are stumbling
through this life, groping in the dark, with little or no
direction and purpose. Jesus said, 'I am the light of the
world; he who follows me will not walk in darkness, but
will have the light of life' (John 6:48–51; 7:37; 14:6; 8:12).
Many are living under stress and conscious of the terrifying pressures of our modern world. Jesus said, 'Come to
me, all who labour and are heavy laden, and I will give
you rest' (Matthew 11:28). Many feel that they can do

nothing of ultimate value. Jesus said, 'I am the vine, you are the branches. He who abides in me ... bears much fruit' (John 15:5). All of us, one day, must face death and life after death. Jesus said, 'I am the resurrection and the life; he who believes in me ... shall never die' (John 11:25–26). 'I am the good shepherd ... and I give ... eternal life'. 'I am the door; if anyone enters by me, he will be saved' (John 11:25–26; 10:14, 27–29).

So we could multiply examples. And yet some say that he was no more than a good religious teacher!

DIRECT CLAIMS

In John 10:30 Christ said, 'I and the Father are one', meaning 'one in substance'. And it is perfectly clear that the Jews knew how to interpret this because in the next verse we read 'they took up stones ... again to stone him'. Stoning was the penalty for blasphemy and if Christ's words were not true then he was clearly an outrageous blasphemer.

In John 14:9 Christ said, 'He who has seen me has seen the Father'. The context of this is important. Philip, together with the other disciples, had various doubts about the person of Christ. 'Lord, show us the Father, and we shall be satisfied.' In other words, he was asking to see the reality of God before he could fully trust himself to Jesus Christ. This was not just an academic question: Philip and the others were in earnest. They meant business. They realised that, if they were to follow Christ at all, theirs must be nothing less than a wholehearted discipleship, whatever the cost might be. Christ had just told them that there would come a time when they would be tested and persecuted; that one of their number would betray him: and that he himself would be crucified. He went on to tell them not to worry about these things, and spoke to them of the certainty of heaven. Wonderfully comforting words! But the disciples' reaction is understandable and indeed, contemporary: 'Unless I can be quite sure, why on earth should I commit myself to this way of life, let alone to a person, to one who is going to be martyred, to one who tells me that I, too, may be martyred, and that anyway I must put him first! That is quite a lot to stomach! I don't mind coming to church occasionally, saying my prayers, helping my neighbour. But I'm not at all sure about getting really involved with Christ, whatever the cost might be.'

I think that something like this was going on in the mind of Philip when he said, 'Show us the Father and we shall be satisfied'. It was a fair question, and it is a fair question today. In some parts of the world it is not at all easy for the man or woman who becomes a Christian:

I myself was later in prison, together with souls whom God had helped me to win for Christ. I was in the same cell with one who had left behind six children and who was now in prison for his Christian faith. His wife and children were starving. He might never see them again. I asked him: 'Have you any resentment against me that I brought you to Christ and because of this your family is in such misery?' He said: 'I have no words to express my thankfulness that you have brought me to the wonderful Saviour. I would never have it another way.'

R. Wurmbrand: *Tortured for Christ*
Hodder & Stoughton, 1967

Of course, we may not face such a situation at the moment. Nevertheless, an active, committed Christian, unashamed of Christ, speaking to others about him, is today very much out on a limb. As one young writer has expressed it:

England has been officially Christian for more than fifteen hundred years. Our whole culture is based on Christianity. However, today it is apparently no longer respectable, or even acceptable, actually to *be* a Christian. This is especially so among people of my own age and type.
Humanism is the thing. It is not that religion in general is out. Roman Catholics are just all right because one is generally born a Catholic and so cannot do anything about it. Mormons are o.k. too, not to *be*, but for sociological study purposes. The Eastern religions are very trendy. But as for ordinary God-fearing, Bible-reading, Christ-imitating Christianity – it's plain old-fashioned. You're barmy, a freak, if you believe it in these days.

Weekend Telegraph

That is a widespread viewpoint. Today, people are very interested to hear about the Christian faith, but very unwilling to commit themselves personally. Why? Because today it is not easy to be a true disciple of Jesus Christ.

You are a marked man, or woman. It costs something.

That is why Philip's question is so relevant: 'Show us the Father and we shall be satisfied.' We want to be sure. And Christ replied, 'He who has seen me has seen the Father'. That is a wonderful statement! At last we can know something about God, because here is a man who *is* God!

Perhaps the most important of all his direct claims comes in John 8, where Jesus is in controversy with the Jews. 'Your father Abraham rejoiced that he was to see my day; he saw it and was glad,' said Jesus. 'You are not yet fifty years old', they protested, 'and have you seen Abraham?' Christ replied, 'Truly, truly, I say to you, before Abraham was, I am'. And immediately the Jews took up stones to stone him to death. That 'I AM' was God's own name, revealed to Moses (Exodus 3:13–15) yet Jesus calmly took this divine title for himself. Nothing could have been clearer. In the words of the late William Temple: 'It is now recognised that the one Christ for whose existence there is any evidence at all is a miraculous figure making stupendous claims.'

And yet some say that he was no more than a good religious teacher.

His character

His claims were supported at every point by his character. As Tennyson said, 'His character was more wonderful than the greatest miracle'. We could spend a long time looking at his poise, his majesty, his love, his humility, his thoughtfulness, his devotion. Wherever he went he cared for the lonely, the sick, the social outcasts, and all in need. No one can fail to admire the beauty of his character; but there is one feature which makes him unique, and that is his sinlessness. This is so remarkable that we should ask a number of witnesses for their evidence.

Let us ask his close friends. They were with him constantly for nearly three years, and saw him tired, tested and besieged by the crowds to the point of distraction. Yet Peter said that he was 'without blemish or spot'; 'he committed no sin; no guile was found on his lips' (1 Peter 1:19; 2:22). John said, 'If we say we have no sin, we deceive ourselves . . .' but of Jesus he said, 'In him there is no sin' (1 John 1:8; 2:5). This is the testimony of two of his closest friends, and such close friends usually know the truth about us!

Let us ask his enemies. Of course, some of them engaged in a good deal of political mud-slinging. Some called him a Sabbath-breaker, a 'wine-bibber', a subversive element, the friend of those whom society had rejected. Yet what happened when they were called upon seriously to examine his character? On one occasion Christ asked his critics, 'Which of you convicts me of sin?' (John 8:46). No one could answer. Pilate said, after careful examination, 'I did not find this man guilty of any of your charges against him' (Luke 23:14).

Let us then ask Christ himself. He, indeed, would be guilty of sublime arrogance had anyone been able to show that his claims were false, but no one could. 'I always do what is pleasing to him' (John 8:29). He was continually telling others to repent, yet he never repented himself. He was always accusing the Pharisees of hearts that were dirty and full of sin, and yet Christ himself had 'a conscience unclouded by the memory of any sin'. Think how quickly these fantastic claims would have been challenged if they had not been genuine.

This at once puts him in a class utterly distinct, not only from sinners, but also from saints. It is the universal experience of all godly men that the nearer they come to God, the more aware they are of sin:

> *And they who fain would serve Thee best*
> *Are conscious most of wrong within.*
> H. Twells

Not so Jesus Christ. As C. S. Lewis put it: 'The discrepancy between the depth, sincerity, and may I say, the shrewdness of his moral teaching, and the rampant megalomania which must lie behind his theological teaching unless he is God, has never been got over.' And yet some say that he was no more than a good religious teacher.

It should be fairly obvious by now that this is the one way in which we cannot describe Jesus Christ. No one in the Gospels ever thought that he was just a man or a

marvellous teacher, because this was an impossible conclusion. To be accurate, there was one person who tried to
say this – the rich young ruler. 'Good Teacher,' he said,
'what must I do to inherit eternal life?' And at once Christ
came back at him: 'Why do you call me good? No one is
good but God alone' (Mark 10:17–18). In other words,
'good teacher' is an impossible description. He was saying:
'Either I am just a teacher, and in that case I am not good
in God's eyes; I am a sinner like everyone else. Or, I am
good, because I am God.' Therefore Christ was either very
much more than a 'good teacher' or very much less. He
cannot be damned with faint praise! He can be called evil,
deluded, devil-possessed, a madman, a blasphemer. Some
called him precisely these things in his own day. But such
judgments as these, when set against his character and
teaching, tell us less about Christ than about the people
who made them. To them Jesus said, 'By your words you
will be condemned' (Matthew 12:37).

Who then is Jesus Christ? We have to be careful how
we answer this because it is a boomerang question; it is
not primarily an academic matter. Some people think that
they can sit down and discuss the Christian faith as they
might discuss a scientific hypothesis. This is not so. God
does not prove his existence by a series of propositions; he
reveals himself in a person, and the way in which we
respond to a living person is very different, and much
more demanding, than our response to a logical proposition. 'Christ's teaching therefore cannot be grasped by
the intelligence', wrote C. S. Lewis, 'cannot be "got up"
as if it were a subject ... he will not be, in the way we
want, "pinned down". The attempt is (again I mean no
irreverence), like trying to bottle a sunbeam.'

Primarily this is a moral issue, a challenge to the will.
Paul said that judgment would come upon 'those who do
not know God and who do not obey the gospel of our
Lord Jesus' (2 Thessalonians 1:8). Therefore, the question is ultimately not one of understanding, but one of
obeying. A Christian is called a 'disciple': one who follows
Jesus, listens to him and obeys him.

People commonly ask the wrong questions about the
Christian faith. Is it helpful? Is it satisfying? Is it worth my

while? These are relatively unimportant. The vital issue is: *Is it true?* And Christ replies, 'I am ... the Truth ... no one comes to the Father but by me' (John 14:6). Therefore, one who wants to know about God and find him as a real person in his life must come to Jesus. He alone can bring him into a living relationship with God himself.

People often say to me, 'But it requires tremendous faith to believe all that! You cannot prove it conclusively. It goes far beyond logic and reason. Perhaps you are wrong.' One cannot in fact prove, logically, any person's existence, even one's own; it is a matter of experience. The Christian belief is therefore a step of faith, and it cannot be proved mathematically or scientifically. But it needs far greater faith to believe that Christianity is not true; that the historical facts of the Christian faith are fairy tales, that Christ's teaching is false; and that the experience of Christians all down the centuries has been based on a delusion.

There is a mass of evidence for what the Christian believes. But where is the evidence for the agnostic position? He has to believe, with the authority only of his personal opinion, that all that Christ taught was either not true or not important. Christ, with his life and actions supporting all that he said, stressed repeatedly that his teaching was authoritative and urgent. Any man who tries to think honestly must ask himself what it was that made Christ speak with such authority and why his message is so relevant for the modern world.

CHAPTER TWO

Sin: a Christian neurosis?

We shall see something of the relevance of Christ if we look at the story of one likeable rebel, the young woman of Samaria, whose meeting with Christ is recorded in John 4.

Like many of her generation she was disillusioned because she saw that the established traditional life of her country had nothing to offer her that was real and satisfying. Socially, the Jews were not on speaking terms with the Samaritans. Social and racial distinctions were deep rooted. Politically, the country, under the Roman government, was 'going to the dogs'. Economically, times were hard; and here she was, poor thing, having to collect water every day from the only tap in the neighbourhood! Morally, there was a hypocritical veneer of respectability! The very people who complained about the morality of her generation were by no means innocent themselves, and sometimes a really juicy bit of aristocratic scandal would hit the headlines. Spiritually, of course, the country was dead. Theologians spent their time arguing whether God ought to be worshipped in Samaria or in Jerusalem. They were hopelessly out of touch with real life, and their teaching was completely irrelevant. I think she would have enjoyed William Temple's definition of a theologian as 'a man who spends his time answering questions that nobody is asking.' In particular, she could not stand the religious preoccupation with sin, always so guilt-ridden and introspective. 'Positively a neurosis,' she might have said. 'What's the point of being morbid all the time? Life's bleak enough as it is!'

The answer? Well, of course, to throw religion overboard. She was no fool. She was determined to get some kick out of life in a set-up which was otherwise extremely dreary. Unless she found some excitement, life was scarcely worth living. Therefore she let go some of her inhibitions, experimented with free love, and drew a large circle of friends. Three words more or less summed up her total ambition: *happiness, freedom, life*. That, perhaps, is a fair description of what most people are looking for today.

DISILLUSIONED

However, she met with a number of surprises. In the first place, *her pursuit of happiness left her curiously unhappy and dissatisfied*. Playing around with men merely convinced her that most men were selfish creatures, out to satisfy their own lusts but knowing very little about love. Further, her search for happiness proved to be increasingly frustrating. Free love soon lost its initial thrill, and left a great deal of pain and sorrow behind it. The wide circle of 'friends' proved to be unreliable and selfish; she was still horribly lonely at times; she had no one to whom she could turn. Nor could she finally throw overboard all notions of God. There were various questions which still required an answer; and there was something else, a conscience, which nagged – maybe not very often, but every now and then, when she was in one of her more reflective moods. She had very little peace in her heart, although you might not have guessed it on casual acquaintance. In short, she was not particularly happy.

Of course, she was beginning to discover, the hard way, the truth about human nature. William Golding is one of today's writers who, in his book *The Lord of the Flies*, reminds us what human nature is really like. For too long we 'have never looked further than the rash appearing on the skin'; it is time we began to look 'for the root of the disease instead of describing the symptoms'. Therefore in his writings he lifts the lid and peers inside. He is not concerned with the externals: what man would like to be and what he tries to be in front of other people. He is concerned, as God is, with what man is like in his innermost being, in the secret of his heart. And he shows us, undeniably, that beneath the surface of our much-prized rationality there is a 'seething cauldron of untamed desire'. Yet, when we see this extremely unattractive picture, it is extraordinary how we try to talk ourselves out of it. We talk about inhibitions, complexes, twists in our nature, mistakes, and temperament. We do not like using the word which the Bible uses, and which Christ frequently used: *sin.*

Sometimes I hear the protest: 'I don't understand this concept of sin. I don't know what you mean.' However, it is also my experience that no one has any real problem about this concept. Everyone knows what it is to be selfish, to lie, hate, steal, cheat, lust, criticise and judge other people.

Paul wrote:

You therefore have no defence – you who sit in judgment, whoever you may be – for in judging your fellow-man you condemn yourself, since you, the judge, are equally guilty. It is admitted that God's judgment is rightly passed upon all who commit such crimes as these; and do you imagine – you who pass judgment on the guilty while committing the same crimes yourself – do you imagine that you, any more than they, will escape the judgment of God?

Romans 2:1–3 NEB

This is a common fault today – blaming someone else. 'It's them!' 'It's him!' 'It's her!' But it's never 'me'! C. S. Lewis, in his book *The Great Divorce*, talks about a meeting with a 'tousle-headed poet':

He appeared to be a singularly ill-used man. His parents had never appreciated him and none of the five schools at which he had been educated seemed to have made any provision for a talent and temperament such as his. To make matters worse he had been exactly the sort of boy in whose case the examination system works out with the maximum unfairness and absurdity. It was not until he reached the university that he began to recognise that all these injustices did not come by chance but were the inevitable results of our economic system. Capitalism did not merely enslave the workers, it also vitiated taste and vulgarised intellect: hence our educational system and hence a lack of 'Recognition' for new genius. This discovery had made him a Communist ... There were money troubles. His father, who had never progressed beyond the most atrocious mental complacency and smugness of the Victorian epoch, was giving him a ludicrously inadequate allowance. And he had been very badly treated by a girl too. He had thought her a really civilised and adult personality, and then she had unexpectedly revealed that she was a mass of bourgeois prejudices and monogamic instincts. Jealousy, possessiveness, was a quality he particularly disliked. She had even shown herself, at the end, to be mean about money. That was the last straw...

It's him! It's her! It's them! *But it's never me!*

That is why the word *sin* is so unpopular. It is too personal. Once I accept the concept of sin, I have to face up to the fact that I am responsible for my actions. I am guilty, and I need to be forgiven.

Christ taught a good deal about sin. He saw it as man's number one need for God. He saw it as corrupting and spoiling the life of every person born into the world. That is why he came: to 'save his people from their sins' (Matthew 1:21). He knew that unless the diagnosis of man was known and accepted, and unless the surgeon's knife could do its work, this cancer of sin would spread and kill.

Yet is it not incredible that some people are still optimistic about the quality of human nature? If we look back over history, every civilisation has boasted of the achievements and abilities of man. We read of the Age of Enlightenment, the Age of Reason, the Golden Age. In the words of Professor James Stewart, 'The renaissance humanists thought that man was the measure of all things. His will was the architect of destiny. His intelligence, storming the secrets of the universe, had occupied the throne of God. "Thou art smitten, thou God", shouted Swinburne vociferously:

> Thou art smitten; thy death is upon thee, O Lord.
> And the love song of earth, as thou diest, resounds through
>   the wind of her wings –
> Glory to man in the highest! for man is the master of
>   things.

Is man really the master of things? Look at Vietnam, Rhodesia, South Africa, China, race riots ... and yet today we find the same silly optimism. Humanists say that man is well able to cope with himself and with the problems of the world, provided that he is not shackled by the immature creeds of religion. It is worth pointing out that humanism flourishes *only* in intellectual circles, where it is *easy* to be idealistic about life. As a minister, I am constantly faced with complex human and domestic problems; and in this ordinary world of needy men and women, although many strange beliefs exist, I scarcely ever encounter a convinced humanist. Once you step out of an intellectual greenhouse into the fierce storms of everyday life, you are forced to be realistic about human nature. You cannot be blind to the sin which exists in the heart of man. Dr C. E. M. Joad, who for many years embraced a 'rational-optimist philosophy', found his idealistic beliefs shattered in the last world war. He came to see that:

... evil is endemic in man, and that the Christian doctrine of original sin expresses a deep and essential insight into human nature. Therefore, for the first time in my life the existence of God in the world made its impact upon me as a positive and obtrusive fact.

There was a famous correspondence in *The Times* 'What's wrong with the world?' Probably the most penetrating of all the letters was from G. K. Chesterton: 'Dear Sir, I am. Yours sincerely.' That is precisely the answer. The heart of the human problem is the problem of the human heart. People have a variety of theories about 'what is wrong with the world', but no one can truthfully answer this question until he can say with honesty 'Dear Sir, *I am.*' Christ described human nature in these words:

From inside, out of a man's heart, come evil thoughts, acts of fornication, of theft, murder, adultery, ruthless greed and malice; fraud, indecency, envy, slander, arrogance, and folly; these evil things all come from inside, and they defile the man.

Mark 7:21-23 NEB

Paul summed it up with a quotation from the Old Testament: 'All have turned aside, together they have gone wrong; no one does good, not even one' (Romans 3:12). Here 'gone wrong' means 'gone sour', like milk, or bad, like fruit – become rotten or putrid. Paul is therefore saying that human nature on its own, without Christ, is corrupt and useless in the sight of God.

One aspect of man's nature is reflected in the widespread feeling today that we can play with God's gift of sex. 'Why shouldn't I go to bed with a girl if I want to?' is a question that I am often asked in university circles. The first answer to that question is: because you are not a self-created being, responsible only to yourself. You are created by God and responsible to God:

We shall all stand before God's tribunal. For Scripture says, 'As I live, says the Lord, to me every knee shall bow and every tongue acknowledge God'. So, you see, each of us will have to answer for himself.

Romans 14:10-12 NEB

Any complicated piece of machinery has with it the maker's instructions, and if these are ignored, the user has only himself to blame if things go wrong. God's laws are our Maker's instructions; we cannot toss them on one side as irrelevant nonsense without suffering the consequences. Some try to do so, but often with tragic results.

That is what the woman of Samaria found; she played with sex, and ignored her Maker's instructions. But her pursuit of happiness left her unhappy and dissatisfied.

FRUSTRATED

In the second place, *her pursuit of freedom left her bound and enslaved to a way of life from which she many times longed to be free*. There is an extremely revealing comment on this woman's life. Christ exposes her sordid sex life, and she goes away to tell her friends: 'Come, see a man who told me *all that I ever did*.' Yet Christ had only talked about her abortive and miserable relationships with men. In other words, this *was* her life, and she was enslaved to it. In one way or another this enslavement is what always happens. We never find the freedom we want until we find it in Jesus Christ. Freedom, apart from him, is a pure myth and delusion.

Ask the prodigal son: a man fed up with the stuffy rules of his father's house; who rebelled in order to be independent and free. It is worth looking at this story for a moment (*cf* Luke 15:11*f*). The son tells his father that it is time for him to leave; so he takes his inheritance and goes on his way to lead his life and spend his money and waste his time, just as he wants, in his own way. The father says not a word, and lets his son go. What does the young man find in this bid for freedom? Much the same as the Samaritan woman. But there are three disturbing factors as the weeks and months go by.

First, he can never quite get out of his mind the memory of his father. He keeps on hearing his voice, seeing his face, and remembering his grief when he left home. He cannot quite free himself from these pricks of conscience. There is no silencer for the conscience on the market. Kafka, whom W. H. Auden insists is the most representative writer of the twentieth century, brings out in his novels *The Trial* and *The Castle* the fear of guilty men in relation to God. At one moment we desire to find God; in the next, we try to flee from him. We protest violently that we want to be left alone, and yet being left alone is the very thing we most dread. In his love God will not leave us alone without doing his utmost to reach us. In Francis Thompson's famous words in *The Hound of Heaven*:

> *I fled Him, down the nights and down the days;*
> *I fled Him, down the arches of the years;*
> *I fled Him, down the labyrinthine ways*
> *Of my own mind; and in the midst of tears*
> *I hid from Him, and under running laughter.*

It is quite impossible to run away from God or to hide from his presence; wherever we are, he can reach us through our conscience, and our conscience always stays with us, whether we like it or not. But the young prodigal does not stop to think about that.

Secondly, he cannot get away from the fact that everything he has – clothes, food, money, possessions – comes from his father. The trouble is that he is trying to live his life without any reference to his father at all, and this spoils everything he does. He goes out to parties, but they do not satisfy him. He has a free and easy time with girls, but they give no lasting pleasure. He makes many friends, but they turn out to be fair-weather friends. That is always the trouble when we live in God's world without reference to God, and use his gifts without reference to the Giver. It does not and cannot satisfy: life becomes hollow and empty and pointless. But the young man does not stop to think about that.

Thirdly, he is not quite as free as he had imagined. He is gripped by boredom, and therefore must amuse himself. He is ruled by his natural desires, and therefore must indulge them. He is bound by the opinion of others, by the longing for popularity, by the fear of what others think; and therefore he must do this and that and the other. He is not free at all! Part One of the story of the prodigal ends with the young man penniless, starving, sitting in a pigsty feeding the pigs.

When a person tries to run away from God, he throws away the real potentiality that God has given him.

Paul says of those who could have found God but who turned away from him: 'God gave them up to their own lusts ... God gave them up to their own dishonourable passions ... God gave them up to a base mind' (Romans 1:24, 26, 28). In the end, God did not run after them, but underlined their own decision and 'gave them up'. George Macdonald has said: 'The one principle of hell is – "I am my own".'

Christ once said 'Every one who commits sin [that is, goes his own way, not God's, in his pursuit of freedom] is a slave to sin' (John 8:34). That is true, although it is part of the wretched deceitfulness of sin that a person may not realise how captive he is until there are crises. A sick person occasionally has an unnatural sense of well-being – *euphoria*. There is also such a thing as spiritual euphoria. Martin Luther, in his book *Bondage of the Will*, writes: 'Scripture sets before us a man who is not only bound, wretched, captive, sick and dead, but who, through the operation of Satan, his lord, adds to his other miseries that of blindness, so that he believes himself to be free, happy, possessed of liberty and ability, whole and alive.'

The Samaritan woman, as she talked with Jesus, began to discover the truth of these words. Jesus said to her, 'Every one who drinks of this water will thirst again' (John 4:13). Yes, she said to herself, this is just like my life: always needing further excitement, always wanting another kick, every day looking for something to satisfy my thirst. That was her second sad surprise: her pursuit of freedom left her enslaved to her desires, always seeking for fresh satisfaction.

CUT OFF
Her situation could be summarised by her third painful

discovery. *Her pursuit of life ended up with mere existence.* She existed physically, but she did not live. She missed altogether the quality of life that God had planned for her. Many people, even famous people with astonishing success in the eyes of the world, have at the end of their lives had the humility to realise that without Christ they have simply existed and never lived. Darwin eventually confessed that by concentrating on only one aspect of life he had lost the power to enjoy poetry and music, and even nature itself. H. G. Wells, having rejected the Christian faith and worked out his own philosophy, admitted that he was utterly baffled and bewildered. His last book, significantly, was called *Mind at the End of its Tether*, and in this he says, '*Homo sapiens* is played out'. A spiritual rebel, despite every apparent promise of happiness, freedom and life, will always find himself cut off from God, the only person who really loves and cares. That is the measure of his success.

CHRIST RELEVANT

What is Christ's relevance in such a situation? After his meeting with her the Samaritan woman could have given us the answer with considerable conviction.

Christ came first of all *not with condemnation or judgment: he came to satisfy and to save.* 'For God sent the Son into the world, not to condemn the world, but that the world might be saved through him' (John 3:17). Of course, there is condemnation and judgment for those who do not want the help that Christ offers. Tragically, the prevailing attitude today is that of sheer apathy. 'Why should I bother?' 'What's the point?' 'Why all the fuss?' This is the answer that the Bible gives: 'This is the judgment' (this is the condemning factor which brings the full wrath of God's judgment) 'that the light has come into the world, and men loved darkness rather than light' (John 3:19). In other words, they said 'Why bother?' Now that is the condemnation! 'He who does not believe is condemned already, because he has not believed in the name of the only Son of God' (John 3:18). A person does not have to be against God before he is in danger of judgment. He simply has to be apathetic: 'I don't greatly care. I'm not honestly bothered. I can get on very well without your help, thank you very much – although, of course, when I am in difficulties I may pray to you, and I shall expect you to rush to my aid.' *That* is the condemnation, says Christ: treating God as your servant.

However, at his first approach Christ came without a note of condemnation, and we see something far more remarkable than a Jewish rabbi talking with a Samaritan woman. We see the Son of God, caring for a sinner, a rebel. Why should *he* bother? That is a question we can never answer. We have gone our own way and broken his commandments and have not cared about him. Why should he bother with any of us? But the fact is that he does!

Christ came, secondly, *not with a dreary set of religious rules, but with life*; 'Whoever drinks of the water that I shall give him will never thirst; the water that I shall give him will become in him a spring of water welling up to eternal life' (John 4:14). I find this wonderful! Eternal life is much more than life after death; it concerns life here and now. It means knowing Christ personally. In the story the woman was looking ahead to the dim and distant future: 'I know that Messiah is coming ... when he comes, he will show us all things' (John 4:25). But Jesus cuts her short and talks about *now*. Christianity is not 'pie-in-the-sky-when-you-die'. Christ brings eternal life now. It is the quality of life that God longs for every person to have. It is like 'a spring of water welling up' inside: fresh, satisfying, quenching every thirst. No wonder the woman replied, 'Sir, give me this water, that I may not thirst'.

Christ came thirdly, *not with a big stick forcing her to obey, yet pressing the point as firmly as he could*. His tone was urgent. He longed to help this needy woman. God will never force a person to act, because he is a God of love and he wants a relationship of love. But while he comes gently and lovingly, he will still press a person hard, because love is urgent, love cares. C. S. Lewis describes this well when he recounts his conversion: 'I had always wanted above all things, not to be "interfered with". I had wanted (mad wish) "to call my soul my own".'

However, God in his love pursued him. He felt:

... the steady unrelenting approach of him whom I so earnestly desired not to meet. That which I greatly feared had at last come upon me. In the Trinity Term of 1929 I gave in, and admitted that God was God, and knelt and prayed: perhaps, that night, the most dejected and reluctant convert in all England. I did not then see what is now the most shining and obvious thing: the divine humility which will accept a convert even on such terms. The prodigal son at least walked home on his own feet. But who can duly adore that Love which will open the high gates to a prodigal who is brought in kicking, struggling, resentful and darting his eyes in every direction for a chance of escape? The words 'compel them to come in' have been so abused by wicked men that we shudder at them; but properly understood they plumb the depth of the divine mercy.

Surprised by Joy Geoffrey Bles, 1967

If an individual feels Christ's compulsion like that, it is because the Saviour longs that he should know the freedom and liberation that he alone can bring.

Finally, Christ brought to the Samaritan woman *not a conventional religious life, but a challenge to be a rebel for Christ's sake.* She had a theological problem (although with her as with many it was far more a theological red herring to stave off the real challenge): 'Our fathers worshipped on this mountain; and you say that in Jerusalem is the place where men ought to worship'. 'No!' Jesus said, in effect, 'don't worry about where you ought to worship. You must worship the Father in spirit and in truth. It is a great spiritual adventure. You can go out every day in touch with your Heavenly Father. He's got plans for you, a job for you. It's exciting, it's life!' And at once she acted. She put her trust in Jesus and then raced off to find her friends, shouting 'Come, see a man...' And they came and they, too, believed. She was already finding the new life that Christ had brought; and it was exhilarating.

CHAPTER THREE

Hell: and a God of love?

John Betjeman, in one of his intriguing poems, describes his thoughts before an operation. He is lying in a hospital in Oxford, listening to the tolling of St Giles' bells. Here are a few lines:

> *Intolerably sad, profound*
> *St Giles' bells are ringing round . . .*
> *Swing up! and give me hope of life,*
> *Swing down! and plunge the surgeon's knife.*
> *I, breathing for a moment, see*
> *Death wing himself away from me*
> *And think, as on this bed I lie,*
> *Is it extinction when I die? . . .*
> *St Giles' bells are asking now*
> *'And hast thou known the Lord, hast thou?'*
> *St Giles' bells, they richly ring*
> *'And was that Lord our Christ the King?'*
> *St Giles' bells they hear me call*
> *'I never knew the Lord at all . . .'*

In the poem he goes on to speak of a vague belief in God that he had because he went to church:

> *Now, lying in the gathering mist*
> *I know that Lord did not exist;*
> *Now, lest this 'I' should cease to be,*
> *Come, real Lord, come quick to me . . .*
> *Almighty Saviour, had I faith,*
> *There'd be no fight with kindly Death . . .*

The poem is called *Before the Anaesthetic*, or *A Real Fright*.

God gives to all of us, from time to time, a fair warning that one day we must die. That is the only certain fact we know about the future. But what then?

> *While I draw this fleeting breath,*
> *When my eyelids close in death,*
> *When I soar to worlds unknown . . .*
> A. M. Toplady

What then? Shall we see him on his 'judgment throne'? or, 'is it extinction when I die?' If I have any sense at all I must know the answer, if I possibly can. It is idiotic to go blindly through life without knowing where I am going, and without greatly caring. Christ taught that there were only two ways through life:

Enter by the narrow gate; for the gate is wide and the way is easy, that leads to destruction, and those who enter by it are many. For the gate is narrow and the way is hard, that leads to life, and those who find it are few.

Matthew 7:13–14

From this, and from many other statements of Christ in the New Testament, he makes it clear that there is such a thing as a judgment to come. 'It is appointed for men to die once, and after that comes judgment' (Hebrews 9:27).

THE RIGHT APPROACH

It is essential that we approach the whole question of judgment with the right attitude of mind.

First, *it is not a matter for idle speculation.* Paul once gave an address on judgment in the intellectual atmosphere of Athens. They asked him to explain what he believed, and we are expressly told in Acts 17:20 that 'the Athenians . . . spent their time in nothing except telling or hearing something new'. Thus, there was nothing they enjoyed more than to sit down, over the Athenian equivalent of a cup of coffee, and toss ideas to and fro, debate them furiously, discuss them far into the night, and then throw them all away! It was great fun: an intellectual exercise, rather like a game of chess, but not, of course, to be taken too seriously!

The safest way to approach any subject which threatens to be serious and personally challenging is to laugh at it, to talk about it with tongue in cheek, and to make all sorts of comments at a purely superficial level. Many do this with God. They make this and that objection, although they do not really believe in any of them; they apparently find satisfaction in trying to fence with God, and to avoid the personal challenge of Christ.

I expect people laughed and mocked at Noah when he

preached to them of God's impending judgment. No doubt they roared with laughter when he built a boat in his back garden. They were perhaps still smiling when it started to rain and went on raining . . . But did they laugh and mock when they were destroyed?

And what did others think of Christ when he wept over Jerusalem because they were blind to their need of him and to the judgment to come? I expect they sneered at that too: 'Rather emotional!' 'Trying to frighten us into faith!' But Christ knew what He was weeping about. It was certainly not an idle speculation, and in AD 70 Jerusalem was besieged and utterly destroyed. Yet Christ also said this about God's final judgment: 'Do not fear those who kill the body but cannot kill the soul; rather fear him who can destroy both soul and body in hell' (Matthew 10:28).

Secondly, *judgment is not an empty threat.* In one of the worst homes that I have visited, the mother used to scream at her children with appalling threats: 'If you don't stop doing that, I'll scratch your eyes out!' It used to make me feel sick, because here were vicious words but an empty threat. But supposing that a mother says to her child, 'Don't go near that fire – you may get burnt', is that an empty threat? No, it is not. It is a realistic warning; it could easily happen. And when Christ repeatedly warns us of the extremely serious consequences of rejecting him, or of neglecting his offer of salvation, because of the judgment to come, is it an empty threat? No, it is not. It is a realistic warning; it could happen.

Thirdly, *it is not a subject that can be ignored.* For some reason, death and judgment are two forbidden themes in conversation today. The fashion is to live life to the full, concentrate on what you can see and touch, and take what excitement you can. Why be morbid and think about death? Why not be realistic and enjoy life now?

It is an interesting reflection that many people today dismiss the Christian faith because, they say, they are being rational and realistic about life. Yet, at the same time, they are being utterly irrational and unrealistic about the only fact of life we can be sure of: that one day we must die.

And what then?

I can never understand why people find the concept of judgment difficult. The idea of accountability is built into the very framework of life. The whole of society would collapse without it. Everywhere we must give an account of our work, time, or money to someone. Why should there be anything odd about the fact that a created being must give an account of his life to his Creator? It is plain common sense.

Paul at Athens found himself speaking to intelligent people and sincere people. He noticed an inscription on one of their altars, 'To an unknown God'. They did at least believe in the probable existence of some god, even though they did not know him in their own experience. And to this intelligent, sincere audience Paul spoke of Christ the Judge (Acts 17:22–31).

INESCAPABLE

Judgment is inescapable because it is universal. God 'has fixed a day on which he will judge the world'. The idea of a world judgment is far from popular especially in these days, and usually there are a number of objections. It may be worth considering some of them.

'What about those who have never heard of Christ?'

This is an extremely common question. The Bible gives two general answers. First, judgment is according to opportunity, so that those with little or no opportunity of learning about Christ will be judged accordingly. At Athens, Paul said 'The times of ignorance God overlooked'. Secondly, in Abraham's words, 'Shall not the Judge of all the earth do right?' (Genesis 18:25). We can leave the matter, with absolute confidence, in his hands.

However, the Bible gives no detailed answer to this question for a very good reason. If a person has a Bible in the first place, or has access to a Bible, then he has heard or he can find out; and the Bible is absolutely clear about his position. The discussion of the destiny of those who have never heard, by those who have heard, is academic. Each of us has to give an account of his own life according to his own opportunities.

'I don't deserve God's judgment'

This is a common protest. We often hear people saying: 'I don't go to church, but I reckon I've got a pretty good chance of heaven, because I live a decent, honest and generous life. My life is just as good as many Christians', if not considerably better!' That is not for any Christian to dispute. By mere human standards it is no doubt true that some unbelievers outshine many believers by the thoughtfulness and kindness of their lives. The only basic difference between a Christian and a non-Christian is that a Christian knows that he needs a Saviour, and has asked Christ personally to be the Saviour that he needs.

The basic sin is that we usurp God's place at the centre of our lives. William Temple once put it like this:

I am the centre of the world I see; where the horizon is, depends on where I stand ... Education may make my self-centredness less disastrous by widening my horizon of interest; so far it is like climbing a tower, which widens the horizon for physical vision, while leaving me still the centre and standard of reference.

Most people, by being the centre of reference for their lives, are saying in effect to Christ, 'Depart from me. I want you to leave me alone. I don't want you to interfere with my life. I want to be king of my own castle. Therefore, depart from me.' If a person says that now, and goes on saying that, is it unfair that Christ should say to that person on the Day of Judgment: 'Depart from me'? It was surely the man's own decision.

'The picture of judgment is much too fanciful for modern man to believe. You cannot expect such mediaeval ideas to live in the twentieth century'

Usually those who make this objection are thinking of those grotesque mediaeval pictures of tortured bodies writhing in a furnace. Such pictures only obscure the real teaching of Christ, and, even more important, do not begin to convey the true severity of hell. This is far greater and more solemn than that of a furnace. Dr J. I. Packer has explained some of the terms which Jesus used when he taught, soberly and deliberately, about hell:

The 'worm' that 'dieth not' (Mark 9:48), an image, it seems, for

the endless dissolution of the personality by a condemning
conscience; 'fire' for the agonising awareness of God's displeasure; 'outer darkness' for knowledge of the loss, not merely of
God, but of all good, and everything that made life seem worth
living; 'gnashing of teeth' for self-condemnation and self-
loathing. These things are, no doubt, unimaginably dreadful,
though those who have been convicted of sin know a little of
their nature. But they are not arbitrary inflictions; they represent rather a conscious growing into the state in which one has
chosen to be. Nobody stands under the wrath of God save those
who have chosen to do so. The essence of God's action in wrath
is to give men what they chose in all its implications ... God is
hereby doing no more than to ratify and confirm judgments
which those whom he 'visits' have already passed on themselves
by the course they have chosen to follow.

This important statement partly answers the next objection, which is the commonest of all.

'Judgment and Hell are incompatible with a God of Love. I believe in a God of Love, who is too merciful to condemn anyone'

On the face of it this seems to be a most powerful objection. However, how can we explain the fact that Christ
(who more than anyone, showed us the love of God) also
spoke to us, more than anyone, of the judgment of God?
Indeed, we can only truly see the wonder of God's love
when it is set in the context of judgment. What is perhaps
the greatest 'love verse' in the whole Bible clearly implies
the possibility of appalling judgment: 'For God so loved
the world that he gave his only Son, that whoever believes
in him should not perish but have eternal life' (John
3:16). The astonishing measure of God's love is seen only
when we admit that we all deserve to perish and to be
excluded from his presence. Yet the depth of his love is
such that we need not, but can know his forgiveness, if
we truly believe on Jesus Christ. Repeatedly and in many
ways we are told that God desires all men to be saved. He
knows that our own inclinations lead us along that broad
road which leads to destruction. Therefore, in his love, he
puts many obstacles in our path: the Bible, Christian
friends, Christian books, and above all the outstretched
arms of Jesus on the cross. If a person rushes past all these,
who is to blame? It is entirely his own fault. God's love is

persistent, but love always risks being rejected. Love can never force, or it would cease to be love. Love will allow the prodigal son to run off on his own and make a mess of his life, even though it longs for him to come home.

It is shallow thinking to imagine the love of God as something weak, soft and indulgent. Absolute love implies absolute purity and absolute holiness: an intense, burning light. 'God is the only comfort', said C. S. Lewis:

He is also the Supreme Terror; the thing we most need, and the thing we most want to hide from. He is our only possible Ally, and we have made ourselves His enemies. Some people talk as if meeting the gaze of Absolute Goodness would be fun. They need to think again.

Most of us disapprove of deceit, theft, bribery, and so on. What would we think of an absolute power in the universe that always turned a blind eye to moral corruption? There would be complete and utter chaos. Unless God detests sin and evil with great loathing, he cannot be a God of Love. As someone has said, 'In a moral universe, all bills must be paid'. The Australian doctor, John Hercus, puts it very shrewdly:

The truth is that men never really have any problem, never any real problem, in understanding the strong, awesome judgment of God. They may complain about it, but they have no difficulty at all in understanding the ruthless judgment that declares that black is black because only the purest white is white. True, we hear from right, left and centre, from ignorant pagans and even from highly-trained theologians, the ignorant prattle about 'All this hell-fire and brimstone talk isn't my idea of God. I think God is a God of love and I don't think He'd hurt a fly!' But it is easy to know why they talk like that; it's because they are terrified of the alternative.

David IVP, 1969

THE ALTERNATIVE

Of course, if this doctrine of hell is not true, then heaven itself is meaningless. How could heaven be heaven if it were full of people who had no time for God? Paul wrote:

Do you not know that the unrighteous will not inherit the kingdom of God? Do not be deceived; neither the immoral, nor idolaters, nor adulterers, nor homosexuals, nor thieves, nor the greedy, nor drunkards, nor revilers, nor robbers will inherit the kingdom of God.

1 Corinthians 6:9–10

The widely accepted theory of universalism, according to which all will one day be in heaven, regardless of their attitude towards God in this life now, is very attractive but, sadly, makes nonsense of heaven itself:

The effects of universalism at a funeral service will be startling. Whether you are conducting a funeral service of a Nero or St Paul, or Eichman or Schweitzer, of Hitler or Niemöller, of an agnostic or Augustine, or an atheist or Athanasius, of Judas or James, you will be able to commit them all equally 'in the sure and certain hope of the resurrection of the dead unto eternal life through Jesus Christ our Lord'.

The astonishing point is that this is quite possible if all have repented and put their trust in God through Jesus Christ; otherwise it makes a sheer mockery of the justice and holiness of Almighty God.

Part of the spiritual blindness of this age is that we have lost sight of the majesty of God. We tend to assume that we are the most important people in the universe, and that God, if he exists at all, is simply there to serve our own requirements. We treat him as little more than our private servant. No wonder we know so little of the true reality of God in our lives!

Further, if the doctrines of judgment and hell are not true, then sin pays. We can be as selfish as we like, we can do what we like, steal, lie and murder ... There is little reason to have any standards at all. Why bother to consider other people?

The cruelty of atheism is hard to believe when man has no faith in the reward of good or the punishment of evil. There is no reason to be human. There is no restraint from the depths of evil which is in man. The communist torturers often said, 'There is no God, no hereafter, no punishment for evil. We can do what we wish.' I have heard one torturer even say, 'I thank God, in whom I don't believe, that I have lived to this hour when I can express all the evil in my heart.' He expressed it in unbelievable brutality and torture inflicted on prisoners.

Wurmbrand: *Tortured for Christ* Hodder & Stoughton, 1967

UNEXPECTED

Perhaps the most outstanding truth which comes in the teaching of Christ about the Day of the Lord is that it will take people by surprise. Paul said to the Athenians, 'God has fixed a day on which he will judge the world'; but

Christ said, 'Of that day and hour no one knows'. It will come 'like a thief in the night'. The great Scots preacher, Robert Murray McCheyne, was once preaching on the coming of Christ and the judgment to follow. He asked his elders one by one before the service, 'Do you think that Christ will come again tonight?' And one by one they all replied, 'No, I don't think so.' Then McCheyne announced his text: 'The Son of Man cometh at an hour that ye think not.'

This suddenness of the final day of judgment is made understandable by the equal suddenness with which death can overtake us as individuals.

One September morning there was a knock on my door. When I opened it I saw a middle-aged couple, very white and shaken. 'Come in,' I said. Slowly they told their story. Their son had gone out on his motor-bike early on the previous Sunday morning. The police said that he had been doing over ninety. He hit a car head on. He was killed instantly; and his sixteen-year-old girl friend was pregnant.

'An hour that ye think not!'

In 1952, the Perth Express crashed into a local train standing in a station. Three minutes later the terrible wreckage was struck by the Manchester Express. In that accident over a hundred people were killed. Underneath the station clock, on the platform overlooking the wreckage, was a poster, with a text on it: PREPARE TO MEET THY GOD.

'At an hour that ye think not!'

As a minister I am constantly visiting bereaved people, and I find that the outstanding reaction is always that of shock. Death, although vaguely expected at some future time, nearly always takes the relatives by surprise. Yet we have so many vivid and personal reminders of the shortness of life and the suddenness of death. In his brilliant Letter from America, after the assassination of President Kennedy, Alistair Cooke quoted at the end two lines from Dylan Thomas:

> *Do not go gentle into that good night;*
> *Rage, rage against the dying of the light.*

How easy it is to go forward into the night of God's

judgment, which Christ called 'outer darkness'. How few rage within themselves until they know that they are ready to meet Christ the Judge.

A young man was ambitious and clever, amazingly successful in business; he spent some time in planning great expansion for the years to come. But one evening he was not very well, and retired to bed early. And in the parable that Christ told about him, God said to him that night: 'Fool! This night your soul is required of you; and the things you have prepared, whose will they be?' (Luke 12:20). He had neglected the one thing that was vital.

Christ expressed the urgency and seriousness of this matter in another dramatic story: about two men, one rich and the other poor. One lived a wonderfully free and independent life, free of all those narrow restrictions of religion, free of God himself. The other, Lazarus, was a poor, pathetic creature in comparison, but he knew and loved the Lord. Both men died: death was almost the only experience, apart from birth, which they had in common. Suddenly there was a great separation. One found himself in heaven, the other in hell. This is how Christ described the feelings of that rich man:

And in Hades, being in torment, he lifted up his eyes, and saw Abraham far off and Lazarus in his bosom. And he called out, 'Father Abraham, have mercy upon me, and send Lazarus to dip the end of his finger in water and cool my tongue; for I am in anguish in this flame.'

Luke 16:23-24

No doubt there was a fine obituary in *The Times*, and I dare say he had a magnificent funeral. But in hell he simply cried out: 'I am in anguish in this flame.' Here, at last, was the agonising awareness of God's displeasure. He at last saw himself as he really was. He knew how empty his life had been, full of worldly things (which he had to leave behind anyway) and empty of God. Christ makes it clear in his teaching that hell is a place of eternal separation from everything good, a place where a person will see that God is right and that he is wrong, and will know at last the glory of God – but that he can never experience it. In this story, Christ talks of 'a great chasm fixed'; there is no second chance after death.

CHAPTER FOUR

The cross: a big mistake?

'One thing at least can be said with certainty about the crucifixion of Christ,' wrote Malcolm Muggeridge:

It was manifestly the most famous death in history. No other death has aroused one-hundredth part of the interest, or been remembered with one-hundredth part of the intensity and concern ... As for Europe, in countries like Italy and France, it is impossible to go a hundred yards anywhere without being confronted with some version or other of the Crucifixion. Since that Golgotha happening, billions upon billions of crucifixes must have been made, from exquisitely-fashioned ones to the most tawdry, gimcrack, mass-produced ones; from huge over-powering Calvaries to little tiny jewelled crucifixes to hang round the neck or over the heart, but always with the same essential characteristics – a man at the last extremity of a cruel death, with lolling head, and feet and hands viciously nailed to a wooden cross.

'The Crucifixion' *Observer*, 26 March 1967

Those last words are important. The cross today is so easily glamorised. It is seen as an ornament round the neck, or a piece of silver in a church. 'How lovely! How beautiful!' we say. But there was nothing lovely or beautiful about the sufferings of Christ. The facts are too horrifying to be told in any detail. Cicero said 'It was the most cruel and shameful of all punishment. Let it never come near the body of a Roman citizen; nay, not even near his thoughts or eyes or ears.' The victim was held down on the cross, while lying on the ground. He was nailed, with fierce, rough nails. He was lifted up and the cross was dropped into a socket in the ground. There he would hang, in intense heat, with unbearable thirst, exposed to the mockery of the crowds. He might stay there for hours until life, slowly and in unthinkable pain, drained away. If ever cruel punishment could be devised for the very worst of criminals, it was this lingering, agonising death by crucifixion. Our English word *excruciating* is derived from the same root. Yet the Apostle Paul could say: 'God forbid that I should boast of anything but the cross of our Lord Jesus Christ' (Galatians 6:14). The teaching of the New Testament and the belief of every true Christian is clear on this point: the cross is the key to everything.

In the Gospel records, one-third is taken up with the passion of Christ: an extraordinary proportion compared with the biography of almost any other man. Christ himself frequently referred to his coming death. He called it 'My hour'. At the Transfiguration of Christ, Moses and Elijah were seen talking with him about 'the death which he was to *accomplish*' – a very strange word to use of one's inpending death. Martin Luther, who struggled all his life to find peace of mind and peace with God, becoming more and more depressed and despairing, suddenly saw the answer. 'If you want to understand the Christian message, you must start with the wounds of Christ.'

CONFUSION

The question is *why*? Why is the cross the Christian's boast and the symbol of the Christian faith? Many intelligent, thinking and even religious people stumble at this centre of Christian doctrine – the crucifixion of Jesus Christ. The novelist, A. S. Byatt, has written:

I was moved by the Christmas story but I rejected the atonement on the grounds that I did not need it, or want it ... God had sent His only begotten Son into the world to die 'for' us but the story did not make it at all clear what 'for' meant.

The God I Want

Many would share his confusion – at one time this was true even of Simon Peter.

Peter could not tolerate any thought of a violent death for his Master. In the Gospels it is quite clear that he was utterly perplexed whenever Christ referred to his coming sufferings. On one occasion Christ asked his disciples, 'Who do you say I am?' (Matthew 16:15*f*). At once Simon Peter answered: 'You are the Messiah, the Son of the living God.' And Jesus replied: 'Simon son of Jonah, you are favoured indeed! You did not learn that from mortal man; it was revealed to you by my heavenly

Father.' Here was a wonderful flash of insight which Peter was given, and immediately he was congratulated by his Master. Then Christ went on to explain the fundamental purpose for which he had come into the world. We are told:

From that time Jesus began to make it clear to his disciples that he had to go to Jerusalem, and there to suffer much from the elders, chief priests, and lawyers; to be put to death and to be raised again on the third day. At this Peter took him by the arm and began to rebuke him: 'Heaven forbid!' he said. 'No, Lord, this shall never happen to you.' Then Jesus turned and said to Peter, 'Away with you, Satan; you are a stumbling-block to me. You think as men think, not as God thinks'.

                                                    Matthew 16:13–23 NEB

'You are favoured indeed!' 'Away with you, Satan': two astonishingly contradictory remarks made to the same person almost within the same breath. But Peter, even with that profound insight into the person of Christ, could not begin to understand the purpose of Christ.

Of course, he and the others had very good reason for their confusion. Like all good Jews of those days, Simon Peter was brought up to believe in a direct connection between suffering and sin. Maybe it was an over-simplification, but the idea was deep-rooted. When Job developed an appalling disease, his 'comforters' were not slow to conclude that his sufferings were plain proof that he had sinned. When the disciples of Jesus found a man born blind, they asked the question, 'Who sinned, this man or his parents?' (John 9:1–2). Therefore, for Christ of all people to suffer was for Simon Peter inconceivable, and his faith and his mind had to do some impossible gymnastics. This could only mean one of two things. Either Christ was not the Son of God, although he had welcomed Peter's acknowledgment that he was; or else God was not on the throne of the universe.

It is not hard to understand Peter's dilemma. At last, he had felt, here was a perfect man, without fault and blameless; God's supreme revelation of himself on earth. And now he was talking about suffering and dying! And death by crucifixion indicated to a Jew that the victim was cursed by God and under the judgment of God. This was common Jewish law. Therefore how could Christ, the Son of God, talk about being crucified? No wonder Peter was puzzled! 'Heaven forbid! No, Lord, this shall never happen to you.'

Again, what could Peter make of Christ's agony in the garden of Gethsemane? There he was overwhelmed with apprehension of the coming events. 'My heart is ready to break with grief,' he said (Mark 14:34 NEB). We can see the confusion in Peter's mind by the stupid way in which he flashed out his sword to defend his Master during the arrest; and once again he was rebuked.

We do not know if Peter saw the crucifixion itself. It is certainly possible, after his pathetic denial. But if he had crept up that hill of Calvary, what could he have made of that hideous sight, and of that cry, 'My God, my God, why hast thou forsaken me?' Was it all a ghastly mistake? Without any doubt his faith in Christ, or in God, or in both, had received a shattering blow.

Indeed, most of the disciples felt the same. On the first Easter Day the risen Christ met two of them on the road to Emmaus. At first they did not recognise him because they were so depressed and dejected. When Christ asked why they were so downcast they spoke of their prophet powerful in speech and action who they had hoped would 'liberate Israel' – but who had been crucified, and buried. They spoke gloomily and without hope of the story of his missing corpse. And at once Christ replied, 'How dull you are! ... How slow to believe all that the prophets said! Was the Messiah not bound to suffer thus before entering upon his glory?' (Luke 24:13–27 NEB).

How dull you are!

When Peter began to understand what it was all about, the fog lifted at once. Everything became clear. 'Of course, of course,' he must have said to himself; 'how slow I've been! How dull I am!'

At last he could see that there was a connection between Christ's sufferings and sin. But it was not Christ's sin that caused his sufferings. It was ours.

ATONEMENT

I have little doubt that Peter did some hard Bible study as

the truth began to dawn. He no doubt thought of that famous Day of Atonement, when the high priest made sacrifices 'because of the uncleannesses of the people of Israel, and because of their transgressions, all their sins' (Leviticus 16:16). It was a very elaborate ceremony. The central moment came when the high priest took a goat, and sacrificed it as a sin-offering for the people. Then he took another goat, dramatically laid his hands upon its head, confessed over it the sins of the people (a symbol of the transference of guilt from them to the animal), and then drove the animal away into the wilderness. The animal was literally a scapegoat, which symbolised the carrying away of the sins of the people (Leviticus 16:15–22).

No doubt Peter thought, too, of the great Passover when an unblemished lamb was taken, and killed, and the blood smeared on the two doorposts and lintel of each house. And provided that the blood of the lamb was applied, God's judgment did not come on that house. The angel of death passed over it.

In both the Passover and the Day of Atonement an animal had to die as a substitute for the people. Perhaps Peter remembered that John the Baptist had once said of Jesus: 'Behold, the Lamb of God, who takes away the sin of the world!' (John 1:29 RSV). The jigsaw was all coming together. 'That's why Jesus died,' Peter must have reckoned. 'He became our substitute. He died in our place. He came to bear the guilt of our sin.' Indeed, Christ's sinlessness, far from disqualifying him from death by crucifixion, became the one essential qualification for becoming our sinbearer:

> *There was no other good enough*
> *To pay the price of sin;*
> *He only could . . .*

Dostoevski once wrote, 'It is not as a child that I believe and confess Jesus Christ. My "hosanna" is born of a furnace of doubt.' After passing through his own furnace of doubt Simon Peter wrote with complete simplicity and clarity:

Well you know that it was no perishable stuff, like gold or silver,

that bought your freedom from the empty folly of your traditional ways. The price was paid in precious blood, as it were of a
lamb without mark or blemish – the blood of Christ.

In his own person he carried our sins to the gallows, so that we
might cease to live for sin and begin to live for righteousness. By
his wounds you have been healed. You were straying like sheep,
but now you have turned towards the Shepherd and Guardian
of your souls.

Christ also died for our sins once and for all. He, the just,
suffered for the unjust, to bring us to God.

1 Peter 1:18-19; 2:24-25; 3:18 NEB

These words, although not a direct quote, have the
unmistakable ring of the famous prophecy of Isaiah:

He was wounded for our transgressions, he was bruised for our
iniquities; upon him was the chastisement that made us whole,
and with his stripes we are healed. All we like sheep have gone
astray; we have turned every one to his own way; and the Lord
has laid on him the iniquity of us all.

Isaiah 53:5–6

However, it is worth looking at the meaning of the
sufferings of Christ a little more closely. Because even
when it is realised that there is some connection between
sin and the sufferings of Christ, many people, including
professing Christians, are still confused about the whole
purpose of the cross. What was the purpose of a lacerated
body, torn and jagged flesh, vicious wounds and excruciating pain? William Miller has expressed it like this:

If anyone said to me, 'I will die for you', I would try to see that
the person was protected from self-destruction. Worse still is the
suggestion that God loves us so much that He dies for us and so
demands our love; if we relate this key Christian belief to our
own lives we can only perceive the most pernicious form of
emotional blackmail.

The God I Want

What was the purpose? Peter gives the answer in five short
words: '*to bring us to God*'.

We shall gain a further understanding of the meaning
of the cross if we look carefully at two cries of Jesus when
he was hanging there at Calvary. First, the agonising cry
of dereliction: 'My God, my God, why hast thou forsaken
me?' By this time three hours had elapsed, an age of

intense agony and stabbing pains. And then came that shattering cry. One thing is certain: Christ's death is far more than a mere example of how to suffer. Indeed, if he died only as an example, we should not be impressed. Thousands of Christian martyrs have shown tremendous joy and ecstasy at the moment of their death. Thomas Bilney, for example, burnt at the stake in 1531, cried out until he died, 'Jesus, I believe! Jesus, I believe! Jesus, I believe!' Yet Jesus himself cried, 'My God, my God, why hast thou forsaken me?' Was he a coward and failure at the last moment? Surely not.

Further, it is totally inadequate to say that Christ died on the cross simply to win our love and allegiance. If someone showed his love for me by jumping into the sea and drowning, I should not be very impressed. In fact, like William Miller, we could only interpret this as 'the most pernicious form of emotional blackmail'. But Christ was doing something far more important than parading his love or demanding ours; he was suffering on that cross a torment which no other martyr could ever endure. He was bearing our sins. He endured, to use one unfashionable word, hell. We cannot begin to imagine what it could mean for God the Father and God the Son, perfectly united for all eternity, suddenly to be separated by the ugly black cloud of sin. That is what happened. In seven stark monosyllables Paul wrote that God 'made him to be sin for us' (2 Corinthians 5:21 AV).

Sidney Carter, in his song *Friday Morning*, has very well expressed the confusion about the cross that is common today. Here are two verses, with one of the thieves speaking:

> *It was on a Friday Morning*
> *That they took me from the cell,*
> *And I saw they had a carpenter*
> *To crucify as well.*
> *You can blame it on Pilate*
> *You can blame it on the Jews*
> *You can blame it on the Devil,*
> *It's God I accuse.*
> *It's God they ought to crucify*
> *Instead of you and me,*
> *I said to the carpenter*

> A-hanging on the tree.
> Now Barabbas was a killer
> And they let Barabbas go.
> But you are being crucified
> For nothing here below.
> But God is up in heaven
> And he doesn't do a thing;
> With a million angels watching
> And they never move a wing.
> It's God they ought to crucify
> Instead of you and me,
> I said to the carpenter
> A-hanging on the tree.

And the astonishing biblical revelation is this: it *was* God they crucified! 'God was in Christ reconciling the world to himself' (2 Corinthians 5:19). God the Father and God the Son are one. You cannot separate them – except on the cross, when Jesus became sin in our place, as our substitute.

The second cry from the cross which may help us to understand the heart of the matter is his last but one. 'It is finished!' In the Greek it is one word, *tetelesthai*. It has been called 'The greatest single word ever uttered'. What did Christ mean by this? Was he saying, pathetically, 'I am finished'? No! It says, 'Jesus cried with a loud voice'. It was a cry of triumph. Finished! Accomplished! The very purpose for which he had come into the world was now fulfilled. The same word was sometimes stamped across bills in those days, and simply means 'paid'. The transaction was finished, completed: there was nothing more to pay.

In the church in York where I am a minister, a tablet commemorates a Canon Faussett who, like a number of clergy of his day, owned land in Ireland. I am told that during one of the potato famines some families on his estate were unable to pay their rents, and wrote, begging him to let them off. He replied that he could not possibly do this: it was wrong, a bad precedent, and he could not possibly make an exception. They must pay their bills to the last penny. However, he enclosed with the letter a slip of paper. It was a cheque, for more than sufficient to cover all that they owed. That is just a tiny picture of what God accomplished in Christ on the cross, in order that we might be forgiven and that his justice might be satisfied.

Paul said to all those who had given themselves to Christ:

You ... God made alive ... having forgiven us all our trespasses, having cancelled the bond which stood against us with its legal demands; this he set aside, nailing it to the cross.

Colossians 2:13–14

It was common practice to nail to the cross of a criminal an account of the crime that he had committed. But nailed to the cross of Christ, what do we find? An account of your sins and mine!

> *It was my pride and hardness*
> *that nailed Him to the tree;*
> *Those cruel nails, O Saviour,*
> *were driven in by me.*

In some deep and thoughtful words of Emil Brunner:

In the Cross of Christ God says to man, 'That is where you ought to be. Jesus My Son hangs there in your stead. His tragedy is the tragedy of your life. You are the rebel who should be hanged on the gallows. But lo, I suffered instead of you, and because of you, because I love you in spite of what you are. My love for you is so great that I meet you there, there on the cross. I cannot meet you anywhere else. You must meet Me there by identifying yourself with the One on the Cross. It is by this identification that I, God, can meet you in Him, saying to you as I say to Him, My beloved Son.'

No wonder Paul said, 'God forbid that I should boast of anything but the cross of our Lord Jesus Christ'.

In the Gospel records, there was a strange and remarkable sign which accompanied this cry from the cross: we are told that the veil in the temple was torn in two from the top to the bottom. By itself this seems to be an extraordinary comment. The veil was a vast curtain separating the Holy of Holies (where God was said to dwell especially) from the rest of the building, and no one could pass through it except the high priest, once a year, with a blood sacrifice. This veil, of course, was a gigantic visual aid, a 'No Entry' sign. It represented the barrier of sin between the people and God. It was a constant reminder that God is holy, and that man cannot saunter into his presence with his hands in his pockets and his life full of sin. Voltaire once said, 'Of course God forgives sin; that's his business'. But there is no 'of course' anywhere in the New Testament. The tremendous Christian revelation is that God can forgive sin, but only through the cross of Jesus Christ.

Many people are only too conscious of this barrier between themselves and God. Prayer means little or nothing to them. The Bible seems a closed book. God is far away, remote and unreal. Isaiah gives the reason for this predicament: 'Your iniquities have made a separation between you and your God, and your sins have hid his face from you so that he does not hear' (59:2). Here is the curtain or barrier of sin. But when Christ died on that cross and when he cried out 'Finished!' the curtain in the temple was torn down. Nothing could have signified more clearly to any Jewish observer that the way into God's presence was now open.

TOO GOOD TO BE TRUE?

Further, it is important to realise that the cross of Christ is completely *sufficient for the sin* of man. 'Christ also died for our sins once and for all', said Peter (1 Peter 3:18). Although the cross happened at a moment in history, it has eternal significance. However, in my experience, there are various deep-rooted questions which are asked repeatedly.

Is there any other way to God and to heaven?

In these days of multi-faith services, the implication is that all roads lead to God, and it does not greatly matter which road you travel on, provided that you are sincere. The answer to this question is clear. If we can get to heaven by good works, why did Christ bother to come into this world at all? If it is possible to be accepted by God through a decent life, why did Christ bother to die? If we can earn forgiveness by being religious, why did Christ bother to suffer the torments of hell? If we can do it by our own efforts, why did Christ bother?

There is no other way to God except by Jesus Christ

and on the grounds of his death on the cross. Christ himself said, 'No one comes to the Father but by me'. Peter said, 'There is salvation in no one else, for there is no other name under heaven given among men, by which we must be saved'. Paul said, 'There is one mediator between God and men, the man Christ Jesus, who gave himself as a ransom for all' (John 14:6; Acts 4:12; 1 Timothy 2:5–6).

This last quotation is especially interesting. In Athens, in those days, if two parties had a quarrel they would present their case to a body of men called 'The Forty'. The forty would then appoint a mediator, whose task was clearly defined: he must faithfully represent both parties, and then bring them together whatever the cost might be to himself. In spiritual terms, Christ alone has represented both the parties of God and man: he alone was both God and man. He alone is the bridge which touches both sides, and he has brought us to God at the infinite cost of his own blood shed on the cross. There is no other way to God at all.

Does it really matter?
Briefly, there is no greater proof of the reality of God's judgment than the cross itself. See Christ's agony, look at the horror of it all, hear that cry of dereliction. there is the reality of judgment! Christ has died to save us from that judgment, but there is a question that no one can answer: 'How shall we escape if we neglect such a great salvation?' (Hebrews 2:3).

Can I come to Christ when I want to?
It is a surprisingly common fallacy that we can treat God, perhaps unconsciously, as our servant, ready at our beck and call. When the convenient moment comes (if it ever does), then we can say to him, 'All right, I am ready for you now. You can come into my life if you want to.' The Bible makes it quite clear who is the Master and who is the servant. 'Seek the Lord while he may be found, call upon him while he is near' (Isaiah 55:6). He is not always to be found; he is not always near. Therefore when he is, it is essential that we take the opportunity while we have it.

God's time is always now. 'Today, when you hear his voice, do not harden your hearts' (Hebrews 3:7–8). If we do not act when we hear God's voice, then we do harden our hearts, and we stand in grave danger of never hearing God's voice again.

But I could never keep it up

This is a common fear. Briefly, the answer is: no, you could never keep it up; but Christ can keep you up. Jude says that he 'is able to keep you from falling' (v24). When you commit your life to Christ, the mighty Spirit of God comes to live in your inmost being. Therefore, you are able to do things which you could never do before. You live the Christian life – with his help! You cannot trust him too much for his courage, his guidance, his love to cast out your fears, his power over temptation and sin.

Is there anything for me to do?

In one sense the answer to that is, No. Everything has been done for you, because Christ has borne our sins once and for all. It is finished! Therefore he offers a free gift, which we simply have to accept. 'The free gift of God is eternal life in Christ Jesus our Lord' (Romans 6:23).

A young boy once sat down with pencil and paper. He wrote down all the sins that were on his conscience: a long and miserable list. Then he took a match and set light to the paper. As he watched the flames burn up the paper he said to himself, 'Christ died for my sins'. And as the breeze blew the ashes into the air he added, 'And he carried my sins right away'. That is the assurance that every Christian can and should have.

CHAPTER FIVE

The resurrection: Christ our contemporary?

'Why is there so little evidence?' Often I am asked that question. 'If this Christian gospel is really true, as you Christians claim, if a belief in Jesus Christ is vital, if my whole future destiny depends on my response to Christ here and now, if Christ is the Way, the Truth, and the Life, and no one comes to the Father but by him, then why is there so little evidence? Why isn't God more convincing? Why doesn't he help us to believe?'

CAUSES OF DOUBT

It is important here to look briefly at the whole question of doubt. Jesus said, in a passage referring to his resurrection, 'Be unbelieving no longer' (John 20:27 NEB). The cause of doubt is not always lack of evidence. There may be plenty of evidence, and yet people doubt. What are the main reasons?

There are few more relevant characters in the New Testament than Thomas the doubter. Today he is probably the most widely accepted patron saint! Now there is something likeable about Thomas: he was absolutely down-to-earth and practical, and he was very honest in his doubts. He refused to say he believed when he frankly did not.

But Thomas had several problems. He was a *pessimist*. When Jesus talked about going back into Judaea, where he was likely to face hot opposition, Thomas, in his typical frame of mind, said 'Let us also go, that we may die with him' (John 11:16). He was always fearing the worst, always looking on the gloomy side of things. Many are held back from a real faith in Christ for precisely the same reason. One part of them wants to believe, another says

'What about my friends? What about my marriage? What about my career? This won't last.' Thus, they are hindered from a true belief in Christ by fear, or sheer pessimism.

Again, Thomas was a *sceptic*. He was over-cautious when he should have believed. Go back to that first Easter Day, and imagine him passing through the dark streets of Jerusalem to the house where the disciples have met together. He is still downcast and sad after the terrible events of the last few days. He comes to the house, knocks on the door, and steps in. All at once he is surrounded by excitement. 'Thomas, we have seen the Lord! We have seen the Lord!' Here are ten Apostles, together with an unknown number of other disciples: all mature, honest and reliable; and all saying with tremendous enthusiasm, 'We've seen the Lord!' But Thomas replies, 'Unless I see in his hands the print of the nails, and place my finger in the mark of the nails, and place my hand in his side, I will not believe' (John 20:25). The force of the original is not 'When I see ... I will believe', but 'Unless I see ... I won't believe'. Why not, Thomas? 'Because I don't understand it and they might possibly be wrong.'

Logically, that is true. But a person will never resolve his doubts if he considers all the logically possible alternatives to faith, or if he waits until he understands it all. How dreary! Where is the adventure of faith? Without this adventure there would be no discoveries: no knowledge of anything, not even of science, and certainly not of God. Confucius said, 'If men spoke only of those things of which they have knowledge, the world would be full of long and majestic silences'.

Thomas was also *disillusioned*. He and the others had pinned their hopes and staked their lives on Jesus Christ. But after all those shattering events, leading up to the crucifixion, they were all terribly disillusioned.

I am constantly meeting people who are disillusioned by what they have seen of the Christian faith in the past. Sandie Shaw once remarked, 'I don't go to church. Well, I mean, you meet such cranky people who do! Church seems to attract them. I'm sure Christianity was all right in the beginning, but not now!' C. S. Lewis made the same complaint, although perhaps in a more sophisticated style:

Though I liked clergymen as I liked bears, I had as little wish to be in the Church as in the zoo. It was, to begin with ... a wearisome 'get-together' affair ... the fussy time-wasting botheration of it all! The bells, the crowds, the umbrellas, the notices, the bustle, the perpetual arranging and organizing. Hymns were (and are) extremely disagreeable to me. Of all musical instruments, I liked (and like) the organ least.

Surprised by Joy Fontana

In 1966 Lord Eccles wrote his book *Half Way to Faith*. Lord Eccles, brought up in the formal and forbidding atmosphere of conventional Christianity, is a confessed unbeliever:

My doubts were increased by the difficulty I had to recognize a professing Christian by his behaviour. I looked round among my believing friends and acquaintances for signs if their faith influenced their conduct. Perhaps I had bad luck, for the experiment was a failure, and what made it particularly depressing was that some of the most unselfish and honourable men, had, as far as I could tell, no religion in them, and certainly never went to church except as a social function.

Further, he clearly received little help from those responsible for his Christian instruction. Concerning an artist whom he admired, he wrote:

He showed me that if I loved a picture at first sight I should afterwards gain a much more valuable understanding of it, than if I had looked at it without emotion, pulled it to pieces and analysed it with all the apparatus of scholarship to help me. He proved to me that love comes first and understanding second. But no one translated this experience into the categories of religion. No one suggested that perhaps this was also the first step towards the knowledge of God.

That is a very shrewd remark. In all deep personal relationships, '*love comes first and understanding second*'. Many people ask far too many questions about the Christian faith. 'When I understand, then I'll believe.' But God says, 'No: believe – and then you will begin to understand'. However, many feel that they simply cannot believe because of the disillusionment they have experienced over the years.

There is, of course, a most important distinction to be borne in mind. Religion and true Christianity are not necessarily the same thing. Neither are nominal Christians and committed Christians to be thought of as the same. Again, the visible congregation and the invisible Church are likely to be different. Christ warned us about this when he said that within the visible Church there would be both wheat and weeds growing together until the Day of Judgment (Matthew 13:24-30). Unfortunately many cannot distinguish the wheat from the weeds. Much of our church life today is certainly a travesty of the teaching of Jesus Christ: full of formality, snobbery and hypocrisy; rejecting the commandments of God in favour of the traditions of men; petty minded, and often ignoring the real needs of the world. This is just what Christ said of the religious leaders of his day. To be disillusioned about these things, however, is no reason for doubting the truth and reality of Christ himself.

Another cause for unbelief is superficial judgment. In his booklet *Unbelief to Faith* (IVP), Stuart Mawson, a Harley Street surgeon, recalls how he came up to Cambridge University and 'began to taste the heady wine of intellectual freedom'. He rebelled against the rules of chastity and the authority of religion; and putting his Bible away, he turned his back on the Church, and 'passionately embraced the "grown up" philosophy of scientific humanism'. And there he stayed throughout his university career and for many years afterwards, convinced 'that the glory of man lay in his courage and determination to make the best of things'.

However, as he became more mature he came to appreciate the limitations of science. You could not measure the love between a man and a woman, or the spirit in a football team; and just possibly the same was true of God himself, if he existed at all. Not everything in life could be reduced to the terms of logic and science. Mawson realised that the scientific method had always been to experiment, and not to rely on the second-hand opinions of others, and therefore, he planned an experiment in the realm of Christian faith. He determined to test Christianity for a whole year to see what it really contained. He soon discovered that he had a deep-rooted prejudice against Christians in general and clergymen in particular! This he felt was basically irrational, but real. Then he took serious measures to investigate Christian belief, and found, to his surprise, that it had a sound intellectual basis. Intellectually it was just as possible to believe as not to believe. It was true that sitting in an armchair one could not prove Christianity, but neither could one disprove it. So the pursuit went on.

Six months went by, but there was no further progress because he had not yet grasped the fact that if God is a person he must be known as a person, experimentally, in a dynamic way. Eventually he came to see that God could be known in Jesus Christ. And the culminating point in his experiment came when deliberately, thoughtfully, trustingly and wholeheartedly he committed his life to Christ. He felt like a scientist on the threshold of a new discovery, not knowing what to expect, and possibly about to make a fool of himself. Christ honoured that experiment. He promises, 'Seek, and you will find'. Here was a man who sought, and he did find. He found Christ to be real and living, and utterly true to his word. He is one of countless Christians who know the reality of Christ's resurrection in their own experience.

FACT OR FANCY

This was the message that absolutely thrilled those first Christians. God had given them overwhelming proof that Jesus Christ was what he claimed to be. His teaching was unsurpassed; his character was a miracle; but God had set his final seal by raising him from the dead! They knew it to be true. The evidence was indisputable. It was a glorious historical fact. And, as Professor Sir Norman Anderson has pointed out, this message is 'either the supreme fact in history or else a gigantic hoax'.

One question, before we go any further: how important is it to believe in a literal resurrection of Jesus Christ from the dead? For some this is an immense supernatural barrier. Christian morality is all very well; being kind, forgiving, generous and thoughtful is good common sense. But why bring in the supernatural? Why introduce the very things which might prove a stumbling-block to the rationalist and scientist? Why not present the resurrection as a beautiful story – a parable, a metaphor, an illustration, teaching profound truth but not literally true? This is clearly a popular view today.

Paul knew the answer to that one: 'If Christ has not been raised [literally] then our preaching is in vain ... we are ... misrepresenting God ... your faith is futile ... you are still in your sins ... those also who have fallen asleep in Christ have perished ... we are of all men most to be pitied' (1 Corinthians 15:14–19).

One man who saw this very clearly a little while ago, was a retired clergyman. During his retirement he read various books on the New Theology, and watched a number of television discussions on the subject of the resurrection. In his old age he felt sure that these highly qualified writers and speakers knew far more than he did, and that when they said there was no literal resurrection of Christ, they must surely be right. That is what he felt. The only trouble was that he knew exactly what this meant. His whole Christian life and ministry had been based on nothing more than a bundle of myths. Fairy tales! He committed suicide. The famous Bible translator, J. B. Phillips, heard about the suicide and, full of righteous anger, sat down and wrote his book *Ring of Truth.* In the foreword he says:

For many years it has been my solid purpose to communicate the truth of the Christian gospel. I am not concerned to distort or dilute the Christian faith so that modern undergraduates, for example, can accept it without a murmur. I am concerned with the truth revealed in and through Jesus Christ ... I do not care a rap what the 'avant-garde' scholars say; I do very much care what God says and does. I have therefore felt compelled to write this book. It is my testimony to the historicity and reliability of the New Testament.

J. B. Phillips, of course, has spent all his life in studying and translating the New Testament. For him the resurrection is a plain, literal, historical fact.

What then is the evidence? We must remember that the New Testament records were written by men whose honesty and integrity stand out a mile. They risked their necks by proclaiming the truth, with great boldness, before the very city crowds which a few weeks before had murdered their Master: 'God has made him both Lord and Christ, this Jesus whom you crucified'; 'God ... raised Jesus whom you killed' (Acts 2:36; 5:30). Naturally they suffered for their boldness. They were imprisoned and beaten, Stephen was killed by stoning, James by the sword. The rulers, we are told, were 'sawn asunder with rage' by their preaching. Could this possibly have been the context of a stupendous hoax?

However, we must look at the facts themselves. There are three outstanding ones.

THE EMPTY TOMB

It is almost impossible to try to recapture the scene of that first Easter morning. Without any doubt the Apostles had been crushed by the shattering events of the crucifixion. Jesus was dead and buried, finished and gone. They had not the slightest ray of hope to dispel their gloom; not the faintest suggestion that somehow, some time, Jesus would rise from the dead. Indeed, the Gospel records make it perfectly clear that when the first disciples came back with the astonishing news that the tomb was empty and Jesus alive, the others would not believe it: 'idle talk', they called it.

Nevertheless, the fact still remained that the tomb was empty. At least five disciples saw it early that Easter morning, and soon it was common knowledge. Further, those first disciples saw the linen cloths lying on the slab where the body should have been, the linen cloths which had been wrapped round the body lying there, undisturbed – but no body.

Now anyone who argues against the resurrection has to find a satisfactory answer to the question, 'what had happened to the body?' There have been plenty of suggestions.

The disciples stole it. But would they honestly have taken the naked body of their Master? Would they really have been so skilful in their deception that the body was never found (notoriously difficult), with the result that they and many of their friends suffered martyrdom, for what they knew all along was a lie? Is there a 'ring of truth' about that?

The Jewish or Roman authorities stole it. What motive would they have had? They had sealed the tomb and set a guard on it to ensure that the body would not be stolen. They were, of course, fanatically opposed to the preaching of the resurrection, so that if they had had the body, they had a trump card to silence the disciples once and for all. But no body could they produce.

Tomb robbers stole it. They were common enough at that time, but what thief would deliberately and carefully leave behind the grave clothes, together with a hundred pounds of precious spices, by far the most valuable possession of the whole tomb?

Jesus never died. He simply fainted, according to this theory, recovered in the cool restfulness of the tomb and escaped from it to show himself as a 'risen' Lord and Master. Is that really possible? Can we possibly believe that a man who staggered on his way to Calvary, hung nailed to the cross for six hours, lost consciousness and then was placed in a stone tomb for three days without food or medical attention, could then revive? Can we accept that in this desperate situation he could escape from his grave clothes and roll back the heavy stone which three women feared was beyond their strength to move, and then walk for miles on lacerated feet? Is that really possible? Even the sceptic Strauss makes the comment:

It is impossible that a being who had stolen half dead out of the sepulchre, who crept about weak and ill, wanting medical treatment, who required bandaging, strengthening, and indulgence, who still at last yielded to His sufferings, could have given the disciples the impression that He was a conqueror over death and the grave, the Prince of Life.

And would Christ, of all people, have created such a monstrous fraud as that?

None of these theories begins to do any justice to the plain facts.

RESURRECTION APPEARANCES

Christ afterwards showed himself to the disciples on at least ten occasions, scattered over a period of six weeks.

He was seen in many places: by the tomb, on the road to Emmaus, in the Upper Room, by the Sea of Galilee, on the hills, in Jerusalem, and on the Mount of Olives. What was it that so completely convinced Simon Peter and turned that utter sorrow after his denial into those forthright and startling declarations on the day of Pentecost? Paul tells us: the risen Christ appeared to him (1 Corinthians 15:5). What was it that so convinced James, the Lord's brother, when he did not believe during Christ's life and ministry? Again, Paul says that the risen Christ appeared to him (1 Corinthians 15:7). What was it that so convinced doubting Thomas, full of demands for visible, tangible proof, pessimistic, sceptical, disbelieving? The risen Christ appeared to him (John 20:24–28). What was it that so persuaded Saul of Tarsus, number one archenemy of the Church? The answer is the same: he himself tells us that the risen Christ appeared to him also (1 Corinthians 15:8).

A critic may say, if he likes, that they were all in a highly emotional state, easy prey to some form of hallucination. But is that likely to have been true? A materialist like Thomas? A hard-headed business man like Matthew? An intelligent doctor like Luke? Down-to-earth, tough fishermen like Andrew, Peter, James and John? A brilliant scholar like Paul? 'Highly emotional'? This would be a monstrous misinterpretation of historical facts!

There was in the appearance of Jesus nothing resembling an hallucination. He could be seen, heard and touched. He could walk. He could show the marks of his sufferings. He could cook fish, and even eat it.

Moreover, Paul tells us that the risen Christ was on one occasion seen by more than five hundred people at once, most of whom were still alive when he wrote and could vouch for the truth of his statement. My first vicar, on the Easter Day after my ordination, did an unusual thing. When he mounted the pulpit to preach his sermon, before uttering a word, he solemnly took a daffodil from a vase by the pulpit, and proceeded to eat it, flower, stalk and all, in front of the congregation! Then he said something like this: 'Suppose you were to go out of the church at the end of the service, and see a man on the other side of the street who had not been here. Suppose you went up to him and said, "The vicar did a most extraordinary thing this morning. He ate a flower in the pulpit!" Suppose the man said, "I don't believe you. I know the vicar, and he would never do a thing like that!" Then suppose that a second person came out of church and said exactly the same thing to this man. And then a third, and then a fourth.

'There must be about two hundred and fifty people in church this morning. The man would be very foolish indeed if he did not believe that this incident occurred after having heard two hundred and fifty people describe it.

'Far more impressive, over five hundred people saw Jesus at one time, and could testify to the truth of what Paul was saying, that Christ was and is alive!'

Sir Edward Clarke KC wrote:

As a lawyer, I have made a prolonged study of the evidence for the events of the first Easter Day. To me the evidence is conclusive, and over and over again in the High Court, I have secured the verdict on evidence not nearly so compelling ... As a lawyer, I accept (the Gospel evidence for the resurrection) unreservedly as the testimony of truthful men to facts that they were able to substantiate.

Tolkien, in his book *Tree and Leaf*, says that the resurrection story:

... has pre-eminently the 'inner consistency of reality'. There is no tale ever told that men would rather find was true and none which so many sceptical men have accepted as true on its own merits ... To reject it leads either to sadness or to wrath.

In 1930 one sceptic, Frank Morison, set out to write a book disproving the resurrection as a groundless myth. But the more he studied the Gospel records, the more he was shaken in his original intention, and the more he was convinced that in fact the resurrection did happen. The book he wrote was very different from the one he had originally planned. It is called *Who Moved the Stone?* and the opening chapter is entitled 'The book that refused to be written'. In the following chapters he goes on to explain 'why that other venture never came to port, what were the hidden rocks upon which it foundered, and how

I landed upon, to me, an unexpected shore' – the shore of
certainty that Jesus was and is alive.

THE WITNESS OF THE HOLY SPIRIT

Christ had told his disciples that after his resurrection and
ascension he would not leave them alone and helpless, but
that he would give them the gift and power of God's Holy
Spirit. He told them to wait in Jerusalem until this
promise had been fulfilled and the gift given, and it is
obvious that at that moment the disciples had not the
slightest wish to witness to Jesus. Indeed, they were timid,
nervous and fearful. They were huddled together behind
locked doors, full of fears and forebodings. They had no
leader, no inspiration, no security – nothing! Never before
had they been so absolutely overwhelmed by the feeling of
helplessness.

But something happened which transformed the whole
scene. The Spirit came upon them. The disciples were
filled with power and boldness. Peter preached: three
thousand people were converted. Everyone was filled with
awe and many miracles were performed. A well-known
cripple was completely healed. Peter preached again:
'You ... killed the Author of life, whom God raised from
the dead ... Repent therefore ... that your sins may be
blotted out' (Acts 3:14–15, 19). Two thousand more were
converted. The opposition grew. The disciples were
threatened and beaten, one was killed, and then another.
But they forged ahead in the power of the Holy Spirit, all
the time testifying that Jesus was alive. Wherever they
went they left abundant evidence that something very
remarkable indeed had happened. So much so that a few
years later, even their avowed opponents described them
as 'these men who have turned the world upside down'
(Acts 17:6).

What explanation is there for historical facts like these –
for the birth and growth of the Christian Church? How
are we to understand these lives which were totally transformed? Take the case of Simon Peter: a craven coward
when Jesus was arrested, but a little later frightened of
nothing and no one! And what of the stories of others?
The power and influence of Jesus Christ, in the world,

century after century up to this present day, has been one of the greatest and most remarkable factors in the history of mankind. Today there are an estimated 950,000,000 believers.

Napoleon once said, with a characteristic blend of conceit and truth:

An extraordinary power of influencing and commanding men has been given to Alexander, Charlemagne and myself. But with us, the presence has been necessary, the eye, the voice, the hands. Whereas Jesus Christ has influenced and commanded his subjects without visible bodily presence for eighteen hundred years.

Sometimes the accusation is made, however, that although this evidence may sound very convincing, Christians are always appealing to the past. They go to the Bible and look at their New Testament. They talk about the events of two thousand years ago. They appeal to Church history, but it is always history. Where is the evidence today? If Jesus is alive today, why doesn't he show himself?

Certainly Christians do go back to the past, because, unlike nearly all other philosophies and religions, Christianity is rooted in historical facts. However, there is plenty of evidence today. I have personally talked to thousands of men and women, from university professors to drug addicts, from top-class scientists to simple country folk: they all give the same evidence, that of the reality of Jesus Christ in their own lives and experience. In Chapter 7 I quote one or two examples.

In one of his most powerful parables, Christ declared that if a person will not accept the abundant evidence that God has given, then even 'if someone should rise from the dead' that person will still not believe! Many people have been honest enough to tell me that they do not believe because they do not want to believe.

However, there is one further piece of evidence about the resurrection of Christ that anyone can have. You can know him yourself. You can find the living Christ in your own experience. You can conduct the sort of experiment that I mentioned earlier in this chapter.

Of course, if this evidence is false, then you must accept

the only alternative conclusion: that the whole of Christianity is a complete and absolute fraud, a terrible deception – and that it has been so for two thousand years.

On the other hand, if this evidence is true (and I would suggest that the facts are conclusive), then it is of the utmost importance that each of us does something about it. Since Christ has risen from the dead, his teaching is true, there is life after death, there is judgment to come, there is a heaven, there is a hell, and Christ is the Son of God. Moreover, he gave this promise: 'I am the resurrection and the life; he who believes in me, though he die, yet shall he live' (John 11:25). We should notice carefully those words 'he who believes in me'. In the New Testament, *to believe* means *to commit oneself personally*. Therefore, our personal commitment to Christ now determines our whole destiny. No one can play with Jesus Christ. No one can keep him at a distance for ever. One day we shall meet him face to face, whether we like it or not, or whether we believe it now or not. At the name of Jesus every knee will bow and every tongue confess that he is Lord (Philippians 2:9–10), and on that day the great question will be: do you know him personally? To many he will have to say with great sadness 'I never knew you: out of my sight!' (Matthew 7:23 NEB).

CHAPTER SIX

The cost:
no life of my own?

In this chapter I want to go one stage further, and make a sober estimate of what it means to become a true Christian. One answer is this: Christ becomes my friend, the greatest friend I could ever have. Now this is the whole purpose of our creation, that we should have a personal relationship with Christ. Until we see Christianity as a friendship with Jesus, we have not begun to understand the heart of it all. I remember what a revelation this was to me as an undergraduate at Cambridge. I had thought of Christianity as an outworn creed, a dreary set of rules, or the habit of church-going, but never realised that Christ wanted to become my own friend. And, indeed, it was not until I had committed my life to him that I came to see what a wonderful friend he could be: a friend who loves and cares, who forgives time and time again, who understands our needs, who feels with us in times of suffering and temptation, who guides and leads, and who never leaves us, whatever may happen. A student at Cambridge said to me recently, 'Jesus is the one permanent object of our trust and affections, in an age that is shifting and temporary'.

One of the greatest compliments ever paid to Christ in the Gospels is that he was called 'a friend of sinners'. It was intended as an insult, but in fact it is a glorious truth. His love and compassion are such that he longs to be the friend of those who are breaking his laws and rebelling against him. Therefore, if at this moment you want to have nothing to do with Christ, he still wants to be your friend! If you are determined to turn your back on him and go your own way, Christ still wants to be your friend. If you are full of arguments and excuses why you don't believe and won't believe, Christ still wants to be your friend. If you are treating him like a servant, keeping him in reserve in case you may one day want him. Christ still wants to be your friend. He is the friend of sinners.

MAKING AN ESTIMATE

In order that we might understand the cost clearly, I want to look at one young man who knew something of his need, and was considering seriously the whole question of his relationship with Christ (Matthew 19:16–22; Mark 10:17–22). He came one day and asked Jesus, 'Good Teacher, what must I do to inherit eternal life?' We could say that he was wanting to make an estimate of what it meant to become a Christian.

Of the many individuals who met with Christ, this was one of the most likeable. Mark tells us that 'Jesus, looking upon him loved him'. There was something which especially warmed the heart of Christ when he saw this splendid young man. Here, surely, was the ideal disciple, one of the few with natural gifts of leadership and initiative: first-class material, someone who could carry the gospel into places of influence; perhaps even someone who could win leaders for Christ.

In a few strokes of the pen, we have a fairly impressive portrait of this young man. He was a *ruler*, which was roughly equivalent to a Member of Parliament in those days. He was *polite* and *respectful*. We see him kneeling before Jesus and calling him 'Teacher'. Jesus, humanly speaking, was only a poor unknown carpenter's son from the insignificant town of Nazareth; a strange itinerant preacher. Yet here was this Member of Parliament kneeling and calling him 'Good Teacher ... Good Master'.

The young man was also *sincere* and *upright*. He claimed that he had observed the Commandments from childhood days, and I do not believe that this was a proud, vain boast, because humbly he went on to ask, 'What do I still lack?' He was ready to admit that he had still something to learn to do. Above all, he was *earnest* and *wise*. His earnestness can be seen in the fact that he publicly *ran* to Jesus and *knelt* before him. His wisdom can be seen in the question he asked: 'What must I do to inherit eternal life?'

You can always tell a wise person, not primarily by the answers he gives, but by the questions he asks. So many today are asking the wrong questions: How can I earn more and work less? How can I be happy? How can I get on? How can I be successful, popular, pretty? These questions may be of some importance, but they are totally irrelevant compared to this first and foremost question about eternal life.

ETERNAL LIFE

What is eternal life? It is so easy for Christians to talk in pious phrases! Is it just singing praises in heaven year after year after year? A perpetual evening service? Even to the most heavenly minded person this would not seem an immensely attractive proposition! The essence of eternal life is its perfect quality, rather than its endless duration. (I am not at all sure that time means anything after death; it is purely a human limitation.) Therefore, eternal life means the life that Christ longs for us to have: 'I have come that men may have life, and may have it in all its fullness' (John 10:10 NEB). Eternal life begins now, as soon as a person finds Christ. It continues even more wonderfully after death.

Perhaps we can only begin to understand the true meaning of life when we have grasped something of the meaning of death. There are three forms of death, and the common factor in each is *separation*.

Physical death. The body is dead, and is separated both from the soul and from people still living on this earth.

Spiritual death. The soul is dead and is separated from God though the body is alive. This, of course, is something we all experience, until we come to Christ. Christ came to bring us to God: that was his great purpose, and the significance of his death and resurrection; and only by these can we have spiritual life, because by nature we are spiritually dead. Our soul is dead to God. Spiritual death is solemn enough; but at least we can do something about it here and now, by accepting Christ as our own Saviour.

Eternal death, when both body and soul are dead and separated from God for ever. And physical death seals our destiny once and for all. Jesus taught clearly that there is no second chance after death whatsoever. When I die physically, I am eternally either dead or alive; either separated from God with appalling finality, having to bear the full righteous judgment of God on my sin, or in the presence of God in a way that is unimaginably wonderful:

Mankind is divided into the righteous and the wicked with no intermediate class. There is good and evil without any middle ground. There is light and darkness without any twilight. There is heaven and hell without any purgatory. Men must choose between life and death, between being saved or lost.

> J. Oswald Sanders: *What of the Unevangelized?*

We do not fully understand what it means to be lost, or to suffer eternal death. But you cannot escape the fact that Christ, who loved us and cared for us, deliberately chose the most solemn words and metaphors to describe the nature of hell.

COSTLY MISTAKES

Coming back to the story, we can see the wisdom of this young man when he asked, 'What must I do to inherit eternal life?' He knew he was asking the one question of absolutely vital importance.

Nevertheless, this story is a tragic one: because the young man, although bursting with promise and potential, made some classic, common mistakes leading to disastrous results.

First, *he underestimated the Godhead of Christ*. He called him 'Good Teacher'. We have discussed Jesus's reply and all that it implied in Chapter 1. We now need to examine those implications as we look at the Christian faith and eternal life. We are discussing the teaching of God.

Someone said to me, when talking about these things, 'I love a religious argument!' But I asked him, 'What is there to argue about? Do you know what happens beyond the grave? Do you know about eternal life and eternal death? Of course you don't!' Thomas and Philip were asking these questions one day. How can we know, they asked, that there is life after death? How can we know that God exists? Because unless we do know, the Christian life frankly is not worth it. To answer both these questions, Jesus pointed emphatically to himself. Do you want to know the way to God, Thomas? 'I am the way, and the truth, and the life; no one comes to the Father, but by me.' Do you want to see the Father, Philip? 'He who has seen me has seen the Father.' In other words, if you want to know about God, and the things of God, said Jesus, you must come to me, you must look to me, you must listen to me. Now that is a very daring thing to say, but again and again Christ spoke and lived 'as one having authority'. Repeatedly we find people holding their breath with astonishment at his words. They were amazed! 'No man ever spoke like this man!' (John 8:46). That was true.

Nor were his claims empty words. Both friend and foe were dumbfounded by the selfless, sinless life of Jesus. Constantly they were astonished as they saw lame men leaping to their feet, blind men seeing, deaf men hearing, the wind and the waves obeying his command. They heard him forgive sins, and command the dead to rise. They even saw him risen from the dead. Someone said:

I am far within the mark when I say that all the armies that ever marched, and all the navies that ever sailed, and all the parliaments that ever sat, and all the kings that ever reigned, put together have not affected the life of man upon earth as has that One Solitary Life.

Moreover, his teaching is perfectly clear. You can open your New Testament and find it on page after page. You cannot push it on one side as irrelevant nonsense. Some try to do so: they give subtle interpretations of Scripture as they read between the lines. C. S. Lewis, in his book *Christian Reflections*, made this comment:

This then is my first bleat. These men [liberal scholars] ask me to believe that they can read between the lines of the old texts; the evidence is their obvious inability to read (in any sense worth discussing) the lines themselves. They claim to see fern seed and can't see an elephant ten yards away in broad daylight.

Therefore, if we approach Christ, like the young man in the story, assuming that he is just a good teacher, we are underestimating his Godhead and we are underestimating his authority. Concerning the supreme question of eternal life, God has spoken through his Son, Jesus Christ.

Then this young man made a second, common mistake: *he overestimated his own goodness.* 'What must *I* do to inherit eternal life?' It seems from the context that he felt, along with a great many others today, that somehow he could earn eternal life. It was almost within his grasp; he had kept the Commandments all his life; so what did he still lack? He obviously felt that he was 'almost there'. This is a terribly common misconception. Often I hear words like these. 'Surely God must accept me. I believe in him, I do my best, I try hard, I sometimes pray and maybe even go to church. What more could he want?'

On 19th December 1923, Arthur Buller's famous limerick first appeared in *Punch*:

> *There was a young lady named Bright,*
> *Whose speed was far faster then light;*
> *She set out one day*
> *In a relative way,*
> *And returned home the previous night.*

This limerick, of course, was trying to capture the spirit of the age: that man was potentially, at least, master of his situation. If he had not yet conquered in every field of knowledge, the triumph was not so far away. Is man really master of his situation? Look at man himself: his nature, his human reactions to other human beings with similar natures and reactions. Lord Eccles writes:

The multitude of new facts and theories does not help us to behave better. Indeed, mankind as a whole tells more lies ... It seems that because it is easier to travel to the moon, it is harder to make men unselfish and truthful.

Halfway to Faith

This is a shrewd and realistic assessment of the fact of human nature, a fact from which no one can escape, and I doubt if there is any doctrine more difficult to deny than the universality of sin. William Temple once said, speaking about salvation, 'All is of God. The only thing of my very own which I contribute to my redemption is the sin from which I need to be redeemed!'

The young ruler underestimated the Godhead of Christ; he overestimated his own goodness; and because of these two errors, *he never estimated the cost of discipleship.* To quote C. S. Lewis again, in *Mere Christianity*:

When I was a child I often had toothache, and I knew that if I went to my mother, she would give me something which would deaden the pain for that night and let me get to sleep. But I did not go to my mother – at least not until the pain became very bad. And the reason why I did not go was this. I did not doubt that she would give me the aspirin; but I knew she would also do something else. I knew she would take me to the dentist next morning! I could not get what I wanted out of her without getting something more, which I did not want. I wanted immediate relief from pain: but I could not get it without having my teeth set permanently right. And I knew those dentists! I knew they started fiddling about with all sorts of other teeth which had not begun to ache. They would not let sleeping dogs lie; if you gave them an inch they took an ell.

All over the world Christ is seen as an immensely attractive person. I find that people are hungry to learn about him, because God has given to everyone a big spiritual appetite, and that appetite will never be satisfied until we have tasted Christ himself. The trouble is that Christ will challenge us about any points in our lives which are not right, for if we want to find Christ, we must give those things up, and allow God to have control. This is always the rub. You may know that there are some things in your life which are causing you trouble, like a bad tooth. Yes, you would like Christ to deal with those things immediately. However, what if he starts touching other parts of your life, which you don't want him to deal with at all? I can simply promise you that he knows what he is doing. He wants you to have the best possible life, and because he loves you, he will not let you go with less than the best.

WHO COMES FIRST?

Kierkegaard once shrewdly put it like this: 'It is so hard to believe because it is so hard to obey.' Most of us have a touch of King Herod about us. Herod was a double-minded man: one half of him liked to hear the truth about God, but the other half did not like the moral implications of that truth. So when John the Baptist was in the maximum security wing of the palace, every now and then he would be brought out of the dungeon to preach in the Royal Chapel. Herod liked to listen to the Word of God. Unfortunately, however, Herod was guilty of a wrong sexual relationship, and every time John the Baptist was bold enough and rash enough to touch on this point in his sermon (and he did this pretty often) back he went to the maximum security wing! No bread or water for three days! 'It is so hard to believe because it is so hard to obey.'

Christ once described in a parable our natural reaction to his authority: 'We do not want this man to reign over us' (Luke 19:14). Isn't that true? Isn't that our immediate reaction? Perhaps you feel that this is a little unfair. 'I don't think I am quite the rebel that you may imagine,' you may say to me. 'I really do want to go with Christ; I really do want to follow his standards and principles in life. I largely agree with the Sermon on the Mount, and so on.' Do you?

Here is a simple test. Where his standards and your desires point in the same direction, there is no problem. But where they clash, who wins? 'Good Teacher,' said this fine young man whom Jesus loved, 'what must I do to inherit eternal life?' I want to go your way. And Christ, in effect, said, 'No, you don't; because when my will points in one direction, and your will points in the other direction, you still want to have your own way.' 'You lack one thing; go, sell what you have, and give to the poor, and you will have treasure in heaven; and come, follow me' (Mark 10:21). There are many who, coming face to face with the challenge of Christ, find themselves saying, 'Of course I want to go with you, but, Lord, I did not realise that this would involve my friendships, my girl friend or boy friend, my ambition and career, my marriage, my time and money. No, Lord, not that!' However, Christ never lowers the standard of discipleship.

In Luke 14 we find him making some extraordinarily chilling remarks:

If anyone comes to me and does not hate his own father and mother and wife and children and brothers and sisters, yes, and even his own life, he cannot be my disciple (v26). This is simply an idiomatic way of saying that our love for Jesus must be so great that love for our nearest and dearest must be as hatred in comparison. Of course, it does not mean that we must give up all our friends. But if there should be a clash of loyalty, Christ unquestionably must come first. If we are not willing for this we cannot be his disciples.

Whoever does not bear his own cross and come after me, cannot be my disciple (v27). This means that we must be willing to go all the way with Christ, whatever it may cost, even martyrdom if need be. Certainly I must be willing for a life of purpose when I lay aside purely selfish pursuits. If we become Christians, Christ has a particular job for each of us to do. Not everyone is called to be a parson or a missionary. We may be called to be Christians in the very jobs that we have so far planned. But wherever we are, and whatever we are doing, we are called to be witnesses to Christ, ready to tell others about him.

Whoever of you does not renounce all that he has cannot be my disciple (v35). This means a policy of 'Christ first' over all that we own. In other words, we must hold everything on an open palm – future, ambitions, possessions, marriage, everything. With everything on an open palm, Christ can take away whatever he wants at any time, and, for that matter, give whatever he wants. What the young man of the story was doing was to close his hand over what he most valued; and Christ said in effect, 'Unless you are willing to open your hand and let your possessions go, you cannot be my disciple' (Luke 14:26–27, 33).

Nevertheless, it is most important to realise that although Christ may demand a great deal (I won't deny that), we simply cannot lose. As Jim Elliott put it, 'He is no fool who gives what he cannot keep, to gain what he cannot lose'. Or, as Christ expressed it, 'Whoever would save his life will lose it; and whoever loses his life for my sake and the gospel's will save it' (Mark 8:35). If you commit yourself to Christ, and put the whole of your life on an open palm, you cannot lose. Yes, he may take something away (which you could not have kept anyway); but in return he will give you many, many things that you cannot lose – especially the gift of himself. He will give you life, and all the riches which go with this. 'Truly,' said Jesus, 'there is no man who has left house or wife or brothers or parents or children, for the sake of the kingdom of God, who will not receive manifold more in this time, and in the age to come eternal life' (Luke

18:29–30). He will help you in your friendships; he will guide you in your career and marriage, provided that you let him have control. What is the alternative? 'What does it profit a man, to gain the whole world and forfeit his life?' (Mark 8:36).

LIFE AT ITS BEST

Some people act as though, if they accept God at all, it can only be on their terms. 'He must prove to me this! He must help me with that! He must not interfere with the other!' We are not God's bosses! We are his servants! He is our God! The astonishing fact is that we can in fact come to him and that we can in fact have his guidance and help. But it must be on his terms. He is God. And again, the amazing thing is this: he is not just lording it over us. In his love he wants the very best for our lives. That is why Christ makes such demands on us as Christians. He offers us all the help, strength, and guidance that we need, but if we are not willing to let Christ have control, he cannot come and do what he wants with us. We must mean business with him.

Maybe I am optimistic, but I believe that a great many people today are wanting, deep down, to know the purpose in life that God has for them. But if we are not willing for that, we have rejected eternal life and consequently chosen eternal death. The choice is ours.

Tragically, it seems that the young man we have been thinking about never stopped to consider this alternative to following Jesus. We are told two things about him.

First, *he was sad*. Mark says, 'His countenance fell', which means Christ had challenged him about the one part of his life which he prized above everything: his treasures and possessions. He was profoundly shocked by what Christ had said.

Secondly, *he went away*. Christ never stopped him; he never ran after him; he never said, 'Let's go fifty-fifty'. It is always all or nothing with Christ. And with infinite sadness, no doubt, Christ let go probably the most outstanding young man that he ever met on this earth. He loved him very much indeed, but love risks being rejected, and on this occasion it was.

CHAPTER SEVEN

Conversion:
escape from reality?

D. H. Lawrence once wrote that no inspiration whatever will get 'weak, impotent, vicious, worthless and rebellious man' beyond his own limits, and therefore Christ's Christianity was doomed to failure. In some ways this was a shrewd and penetrating remark, because D. H. Lawrence was being realistic about man's nature and man's natural inability to fulfil any reasonably demanding code of ethics or philosophy of life. He was not implying that all men are wholly bad and could never do anything good. That is plain nonsense. But he was saying, in effect, that it is no good throwing the Bible, or the Sermon on the Mount, or the Ten Commandments at a person, and saying 'Keep that!' It is quite impossible. Most of us recognise that we cannot live up even to our own standards. And if Christ came merely to underline the Ten Commandments, and intensify their application by referring them to thoughts as well as deeds (which he did), there would be no good news of Christ at all – only a hopeless, legalistic, idealistic, but utterly unrealistic, standard of life, to which no one could ever attain.

This inability of man to live up to a standard set for him pinpoints one of the main differences between Christianity and the other great religions of the world. All other religions say: do this, don't do this, don't do that. They point to a Mount Everest of achievement and say 'That is what you must try to scale by your own determination and discipline'. Christianity, on the other hand, fully recognises, as did D. H. Lawrence, that man, left to himself, is 'weak, impotent, vicious, worthless and rebellious', unable to keep the Ten Commandments, his Maker's instructions. Therefore it provides him not only with the Saviour to deal with the guilt of the past, but a powerful living Spirit to deal with the present and the future. In some famous words of William Temple:

It is no good giving me a play like Hamlet or King Lear, and telling me to write a play like that. Shakespeare could do it; I can't. And it is no good showing me a life like the life of Jesus and telling me to live a life like that. Jesus could do it; I can't. But if the genius of Shakespeare could come and live in me, then I could write plays like that. And if the Spirit of Jesus could come and live in me, I could live a life like that.

That is what Christ had to make clear to Nicodemus, a gifted intellectual who came one night to ask various questions that were on his mind (John 3:1–21). Nicodemus had heard a lot about this astonishing carpenter from Nazareth: how he spoke with authority, healed the sick, cast out demons, and even raised the dead. Why, Jesus was the talking point of the whole city. Here surely was a man who would at last answer the really vital questions on his mind.

Before many minutes, Nicodemus found himself face to face with Jesus. 'Rabbi,' he said with respect (he had his opening speech prepared), 'we know that you are a teacher come from God; for no one can do these signs that you do, unless God is with him.' But Jesus cut him short. The next three words in the story are 'Jesus answered him': strange words, because Nicodemus had so far not asked a single question! But 'Jesus answered him'.

BORN AGAIN

Jesus knows the heart and mind of every single person. He knows the secret thoughts, the hidden desires, the innermost problems. And on this occasion, Jesus was saying, in effect, 'Nicodemus, I know that you have one burning question in your mind; that is why you have come to me. I know there are lots of questions and problems, but above all there is one basic problem: how can God become real to you?' And the answer Jesus gave to Nicodemus was, 'You must be born again'. 'How?' Behind Nicodemus' question lay another, 'Why?' He was a religious man, respectable and upright, a teacher of the Jews, well known in the neighbourhood, and here was this comparatively young man saying to him, of all people, 'You haven't started; you need a new life altogether'. Why?

Jesus gave two clear reasons. First, unless we are born again, we *cannot see the kingdom of God*. A man once stood on a soap-box at Hyde Park Corner, pouring scorn on Christianity. 'People tell me that God exists; but I can't see him. People tell me that there is a life after death; but I can't see it. People tell me that there is a judgment to come; but I can't see it. People tell me that there is a heaven and a hell; but I can't see them...' He won cheap applause, and climbed down from his 'pulpit'. Another struggled on to the soap-box. 'People tell me that there is green grass all round; but I can't see it. People tell me that there is blue sky above; but I can't see it. People tell me that there are trees nearby; but I can't see them. You see, I'm blind!'

Christ made it perfectly clear that unless a man is born again he is spiritually blind. He cannot see the kingdom of God. Nicodemus could not see. He kept asking, 'How? How can this be?' But Nicodemus was not alone in his blindness. He was suffering from a complaint that many have today. The fact is that when it comes to the greatest and most important facts in the world – the existence of God, the way to heaven, the path of happiness now – man is spiritually blind. He is groping in the dark; he does not know where he is going.

A student who was training to be a teacher once came to me and said, 'I have just realised that I am going to influence hundreds of young people in the future. I shall be guiding them one way or another. The trouble is, I do not know which way I am going myself.' He was right to be concerned, because Christ made it clear that ultimately every person can travel in only one of two directions: the narrow path leading to life, or the broad road leading to destruction.

A business man with money, a secure future, a lovely home, an attractive wife and three children, asked me a few years ago, 'What is the whole purpose of life? I have everything at my feet, and yet I do not know the meaning of life.' He was, in fact, beginning to discover that there is no lasting purpose apart from Christ. He was echoing those words of the Lennon and McCartney song:

> He's a real nowhere man,
> Sitting in his nowhere land,
> Making all his nowhere plans for nobody.
> Doesn't have a point of view,
> Knows not where he's going to . . .

Some time ago I received this letter from a young mother:

I will never forget January 13th, 1967, when you helped me to make my big decision (to accept Christ as my Saviour and Lord). During those two weeks you made me understand where I was going ... I was simply going through life like a blind person who didn't even want to see.

This was an honest remark because it reveals one of the commonest causes of spiritual blindness; there are none so blind as those who won't see! However, she went on to say, 'Now it is wonderful to have a Friend so near to me all the time, who watches over me, and listens to me wherever I go.' She had found in life the glorious meaning that Christ can bring.

Malcolm Muggeridge, preaching at Edinburgh in January 1968, said:

I come back ... to the Christian notion that man's efforts to make himself permanently happy are doomed to failure. He must indeed, as Christ said, be born again ... As far as I am concerned, it is Christ or nothing.

Man's spiritual blindness becomes obvious if one listens to a religious conversation amongst those who are not committed Christians; often they refer to God as some vague thing, a subject for debate and argument. We are by nature utterly blind to the fact of God's holiness and majesty; not seeing that in his hand is our very breath and life. Others again stand Christ, as it were, as a prisoner in the dock, while *they* pass their judgment on *him*! Once again, they are blind to the fact that by their verdicts they themselves are being judged.

I remember talking to an intelligent student studying criminology. We talked and talked about the Christian faith, and he just could not see it and could not under-

stand what it was all about. However, the time came
when, humbly and simply, he asked Christ into his life. At
once he saw it! I used to read the Bible with him, and
about a month after he had taken this step of faith he said
to me, 'Now I see it all. I feel like a little child starting
again from scratch.' He was born again. But if this inner
rebirth does not take place a man cannot *see* the kingdom
of God. That is the first statement that Jesus made to
Nicodemus.

Secondly, unless we are born again, we *cannot enter the
kingdom of God*. If we choose to be independent of God, to
go our own way, persistently to break the greatest commandment there is (loving God with all our heart, mind,
soul and strength), then why on earth do we imagine that
we can sail into God's presence when the moment comes?
The truth is, of course, that we cannot. Christ had to go to
the cross and die in our place and bear our sin before we
could possibly come into God's presence. He had to
remove the one great barrier which separates man from
God, the barrier of sin. Christ died to bring us to God.
There is no other way. Apart from the cross of Christ,
there is no hope whatsoever. Therefore, if a person has
chosen to live his life separated from God, then separated
from God he will be! It is his own choice.

Bishop Taylor Smith, former Chaplain-General of the
British Forces, was once preaching in a large cathedral. In
order to emphasise the necessity of this new birth, he said:

My dear people, do not substitute anything for the new birth.
You may be a member of a church, but church membership is
not new birth, and 'except a man be born again, he cannot see
the kingdom of God.'

On his left sat the Archdeacon in his stall. Pointing
directly at him, he said:

You might even be an archdeacon like my friend in his stall and
not be born again, and 'except a man be born again, he cannot
see the kingdom of God'. You might even be a bishop like
myself, and not be born again, and 'except a man be born again,
he cannot see the kingdom of God'.

A day or so later he received a letter from the
Archdeacon, in which he wrote:

My dear Bishop: You have found me out. I have been a clergyman for over thirty years, but I have never known anything of the joy that Christians speak of. I never could understand it. Mine has been a hard, legal service. I did not know what the matter was with me, but when you pointed directly at me, and said, 'You might even be an archdeacon and not be born again', I realised in a moment what the trouble was. I had never known anything of the new birth.

The next day the Bishop and the Archdeacon met and looked at the Bible together; and after some hours, both were on their knees, the Archdeacon taking his place before God as a sinner, and telling Christ that he would trust him as his Saviour. From that moment everything was different. It does not matter who you are: theologian, ordinand, lecturer, minister, bishop; 'you must be born again'. Those are the words of Christ, the Son of God.

A FEW OBJECTIONS

Many people have told me that they make objections as convenient excuses for trying to keep Christ at arm's length, so that they do not have to get involved. To say so is honest. Perhaps the key question is, 'If someone answered all your objections would you accept Christ as your Saviour and Lord?' If the answer is 'No' there is no point in going on. However, clearly there is such a thing as a genuine, honest seeker, and therefore it is right to look briefly at some of the most common difficulties.

I find all this too emotional

Whenever someone levels the charge of emotionalism I am interested to see the person who makes that remark. What is he like? Is he a desiccated intellectual? Has he no emotions at all? Christ is concerned with the whole man: body, mind, heart, and will. To by-pass the mind altogether and whip up the emotions is something I am as much against as anyone else. But true Christianity does not leave the emotions untouched. The only thing which has no emotions is a dead body, and if your faith is without emotion it is a dead faith.

Supposing that someone said, 'I'm frightened of marriage: it is all too emotional!' Well, of course, it involves the emotions! It is the commitment of one's total life to another. It is a terrible marriage if no emotions are involved.

Do not be at all frightened of your emotions when you give your life to Christ; though for many people, this is a comparatively unemotional experience.

I have tried before to be a Christian, but it hasn't worked

I have sympathy if that is your position; you may naturally be hesitant about another step of faith. But it is worth asking two questions. First, did you ever before really ask Christ to come into your life, or did you simply start doing 'Christian' things? You can quite easily turn over a new leaf without beginning a new life. Secondly, if you really did ask Christ to come in, have you gone on with that friendship? Every true friendship needs to be developed and deepened. As soon as you take it for granted, it will fade altogether.

However, if you feel that you have tried before and that it hasn't worked, I would say: 'Don't analyse too carefully what happened or what did not happen in the past. You may have done it, as it were, in pencil already. Now, ink it over. Make it definite.' I have known many people who have come through to a clear personal relationship with Christ by doing just that.

Isn't it presumptuous to be definite and to say that 'my' God is real?

'Isn't it more humble to say that I am seeking for him, trying my best, without being too definite about it?' Of course not! Your eternal future depends on your relationship with God. Of course God wants you to know, beyond any shadow of doubt. The first letter of John was written for this very purpose: 'I write this to you who believe in the name of the Son of God, that you may know that you have eternal life' (1 John 5:13). Throughout the letter John gives very carefully the tests by which a person may know whether or not he has eternal life.

Suppose that you asked me, 'Are you married?' What would you think if I replied, 'Well, I think so. I am doing my best. I wash up the breakfast things, get the coal in, give her the housekeeping money and buy her clothes. Yes' (with a sigh), 'I think I must be married!' That is ridiculous! If you asked me, 'Are you married?' my answer would be 'Yes, because on 19th September 1964, I committed my life, for better for worse; for richer for poorer, to Elizabeth Anne McEwan-Smith; and I have never been the same since!' That is how I know I am married. It is almost exactly the same with being born again. I know I am born again, because on 6th October 1954, I committed my life for better (not for worse), for richer (not for poorer), to Jesus Christ, my Saviour and Lord. I have never been the same since! That is how I know I am born again. It is not presumptuous. God longs for each one of us to know, and to be able to say, 'My God is real'.

I could never keep it up

'I know I would be exactly the same in a few weeks' time.' There are two things to say about this. First, you will never be quite the same if you truly accept Christ into your life. You will be born again, and a member of God's family. You will have a new relationship with God altogether, which is now fixed. John says in his Gospel. 'To all who received him, who believed in his name, he gave power to become children of God' (John 1:12). Secondly, you are not asked to keep up this Christian life in your own strength. The glorious news for the Christian is that Christ is able to keep him from falling. Jesus said, 'I give them eternal life, and they shall never perish, and no one shall snatch them out of my hand' (John 10:28). When you become a Christian, the Spirit of God comes to dwell in your whole being. The same power that raised Jesus from the dead is now in your life. The same power that took away the fear from those first disciples and sent them out with boldness and courage is now with you. You may be afraid of your showing as a Christian in front of your friends. You will never have to stand on your own: the Spirit of God will guide you and help you, if only you let him.

It is not a continuous struggle all the time, for the Christian. The more you rest in Christ's strength, Christ's faithfulness, Christ's love, and Christ's peace, the more he will live out his life in you. He wants to help you all the way, in all your decisions, in matters of guidance, in problems and in difficulties. He comes, as he once said, to give you rest.

The reality of the effects of the Spirit's presence can clearly be seen in the new Testament, and especially in the Acts of the Apostles. When the gift of the Spirit came down upon those first Christians, the whole scene was utterly transformed. The story of the birth and growth of the Christian Church from a tiny band of frightened men and women is quite remarkable. In the words of J. B. Phillips, 'Even if I were not myself a convinced Christian, I should find it impossible to explain this strange phenomenon' (*Ring of Truth* Hodder & Stoughton, 1967).

A university student asked me, a little while ago, 'If all the Bibles in the world were destroyed tomorrow' (I love these hypothetical questions!) 'what evidence would there be for the Christian faith? Is God at work today? Are people born again today? How can I know that Christ is alive? How can we know that God is real?' I could write many books in answer to that. If I did not see the Spirit of God manifestly at work in the lives of individuals week in, week out, I should certainly find it hard to go on preaching the Christian faith with any assurance.

When a person commits himself to Christ and is born again by the Spirit of God, exciting things begin to happen. This is no vague theory. The new birth concerns *life*. This is how Paul put it: 'If any one is in Christ, he is a new creation' (2 Corinthians 5:17). In the Greek it is even more forceful than that. There is no verb in the second part of the sentence, so that it really reads like a startling headline: If any one is in Christ – new creation! Paul goes on, 'the old has passed away, behold, the new has come'. Concerning human nature, Jesus once said, 'Make the tree good, and its fruit good' (Matthew 12:33). Of course! That is obvious! But the problem which has defied man down the ages is, how do you make the tree good? How do you change the human heart? How can you make selfish man unselfish? How can you make a person control his tongue? This is an important question. The Bible rightly says that 'no human being can tame the tongue' (James 3:8). A gipsy once wrote:

No scientist is as sure of the working of any law, no physician is as sure of any medicine, no mathematician is as sure of any axiom, as I am that Jesus Christ came into my gipsy tent and converted my rough, swearing, drinking, pilfering, gipsy father into a clean, tender, honourable, strong, beautiful Christian man.

Temple Gairdner made his personal comment on the words 'behold all things are become new' (2 Corinthians 5:17 AV):

This sense of newness is simply delicious. It makes new the Bible, and friends, and all mankind, and love, and spiritual things, and Sunday, and church, and God himself.

Richard Wurmbrand, having suffered greatly at the hands of communists, speaks of the reality of Christ in a filthy prison cell:

I have seen Christians in communist prisons with fifty pounds of chains on their feet, tortured with red hot iron pokers, in whose throats spoonfuls of salt have been forced being kept afterwards without water, starving, whipped, suffering from cold and praying with fervour for the communists. This is humanly inexplicable! It is the love of Christ which was shed into our hearts...

Tortured for Christ Hodder & Stoughton, 1967

Every week I talk with people, or receive letters from people, who have discovered what it is to be a new creation in Christ, and to know the Spirit of Christ transforming their lives.

There is one further important comment that I must make in this chapter. When Christ says, 'You must be born again', it is not just pious advice. It is not just his own personal opinion. It is a *command*! Christ is the Son of God and the King of kings. He does not say something without meaning it and without urgency and authority. In John 3 there is an interesting, though solemn, progression of statements about Jesus Christ:

Whoever believes in him may have eternal life. (v15)

Whoever believes in him shall not perish. (v16)

He who does not believe is condemned already. (v18)

He who does not obey the Son shall not see life, but the wrath of God rests upon him. (v36)

Step by step we are warned with increasing solemnity and severity. Therefore, says Jesus, 'You must be born again'. Christ knows that one day he must judge the world, and then he will have to underline the decision that each of us has made about him. If you say now, and in the future, 'Depart from me – I do not want you as my Saviour and Lord', then one day he must act on that decision. He will say to you, 'Depart from me!'

But Christ did not come into the world to condemn, but to save. And because he loves us, he says with great urgency and feeling, 'You must be born again'.

CHAPTER EIGHT

Commitment

The question is, how? It is all very well being told 'You must be born again', 'You must come to Christ', 'You must find the reality of God in your experience'. The question is, how? Jesus once said, 'Seek, and you will find'; but there are many who complain that they have sought – at some time or other – but have never found. Here in this final chapter I want to explain, as simply as I can, what it means to find Christ and how it is possible to say 'My God is real'.

FINDING THE REALITY OF GOD

Wherever the first disciples went, they preached one message which could be summarised in two words: *repent* and *believe*. What do these words mean?

Repent

This means 'About Turn', or, more accurately, a change of mind leading to a change of direction. If in any journey you realise that you have been going in the wrong direction, as soon as you turn round and start going in the right direction you begin to make progress.

Therefore, before any person can find Christ, he must humbly admit that he has been going in the wrong direction: 'I've been going *my* own way, doing what *I* want, not what God wants.' If we look at God's laws, or at the teaching and example of Christ himself, it is quite clear that on countless occasions we have not followed his instructions but gone our own way instead – a way, said Christ, which leads us finally to destruction – an eternal separation from God and from everything good.

In practical terms, repentance involves two decisions. First, you must be willing, with the help of Christ, to let go anything which you know is wrong. It may be big or small. But if on any point God touches your conscience or shows you in his Word that something is not right in his eyes, you must be willing to give it up. You may not be able to do so in your own strength. Habits die hard. But if you are willing to let it go, then Christ will help to put that thing right.

Secondly, you must be willing to go with Christ in the future, wherever he may lead you. 'If any man would come after me, let him deny himself and take up his cross and follow me' (Mark 8:34). I have written more fully about this in Chapter 6. But basically it means Christ first – first in your friendships and relationships, first in your job and in your home, first with your money and possessions, first in your love and marriage, first in your ambitions and in your future. The whole of your life must be on an 'open palm', so that Christ can take away what he wants when he wants, and he can give you what he wants when he wants. Let me at once say that he comes to enrich your life at every point; if he takes something away it is only because he has something better in store for you:

For whoever would save his life will lose it; and whoever loses his life for my sake and the gospel's will save it. For what does it profit a man, to gain the whole world and forfeit his life?

Mark 8:35–36

He must also be unashamed of Christ in front of others: not always 'preaching' at them, but openly and unashamedly a true committed Christian.

Believe

There are various truths that a Christian must believe: above all that through Christ's death and resurrection it is possible for us to have a personal relationship with the Living God (see Chapters 4 and 5).

But 'belief' in the New Testament involves action. If I believe in Christ I commit myself unreservedly to him. Any 'belief' short of this is not true Christian belief. James asks in his letter, with a touch of scorn, 'So you believe that there is one God? That's fine. So do all the devils in hell, and shudder in terror!' (James 2:19 (J.B. Phillips)).

One way of illustrating Christian belief is by the

Anglican Marriage Service! When I was married, the minister asked me, 'David, will you have this woman?' I said, 'I will'. Turning to my wife he said, 'Anne, will you have this man?' She said, 'I will'. The moment we *both* said, 'I will', *that* moment a new relationship was fixed and established. Let me now dramatise Christian commitment like this:

'Saviour, will you have this sinner?' Always, on every occasion, no matter who the sinner may be or what sins he has committed, Jesus replies, 'I will'.

The vital question is now, therefore:

'Sinner, will you have this Saviour?' As soon as you say, 'I will', and really mean it, a new relationship will be fixed and established. Through Christ you will be able to say, with increasing conviction and joy, *My God is real*.

This analogy is perhaps useful for two further reasons. First, at my wedding when I said, 'I will', I don't think I had any feelings at all; if anything I felt numb! Similarly when you say 'I will' to Jesus you may feel nothing and be tempted to wonder whether there is any reality at all. Let me stress that feelings are comparatively unimportant at this stage and at every stage of our Christian life. The important point in commitment is an act of *will*, and Christ promises: 'Him who comes to me I *will not* [double negative in the Greek – very strong] cast out.' Trust his Word and believe that you now have a permanent relationship with him.

Secondly, when I said 'I will' at my wedding, this was only the beginning of a new life. Much more was to follow. To be honest, the first year was somewhat rough at times. The new relationship had to be worked out, and many adjustments had to be made. So it is with Christ. This step is only a beginning, but it is a vital beginning.

If you have never taken this step before, or if you are not sure about it, then let me encourage you to 'launch out' if you are ready. As I said earlier, you may have done it in pencil before. Well, there is no harm in inking it over, so that from now on you can be absolutely sure that you have given your life personally to Jesus Christ and that you belong to him for ever. If you are not ready, then don't take this step. But there is an urgency whenever we understand the heart of the Christian message: 'Seek the Lord while he may be found, call upon him while he is near' (Isaiah 55:6). He is not always to be found; he is not always near. We can't pick and choose our moment to come to him.

If, therefore, you have never taken this step, or are not sure and would like to be sure, here is a prayer which you could make your own:

'Lord Jesus Christ, I admit that I have sinned and gone my own way. I am willing to turn from what I know is wrong, and I am willing to follow you and to go wherever you lead. Thank you for dying on the Cross to bear away my sin. And now I come to you, Lord Jesus. I say, "I will". I ask you to be my Saviour and Friend and Lord for ever. Thank you Lord Jesus. Amen.'

PROVING THE REALITY OF GOD

If you have just prayed that prayer then this is the beginning of a new and wonderful friendship with the Lord Jesus which can and must be deepened over the months and years. Let us look at Saul of Tarsus to see what happened to him when he met with the Risen Christ on the road to Damascus and what were some of the immediate consequences of this vital encounter. There are a number of points from Acts 9 which will help you to prove the reality of God in your own personal experience.

He trusted Christ's Word

Now as he journeyed he approached Damascus, and suddenly a light from heaven flashed about him. And he fell to the ground and heard a voice saying to him, 'Saul, Saul, why do you persecute me?' And he said, 'Who are you, Lord?' And he said, 'I am Jesus, whom you are persecuting...'

vv3–5

It is quite clear from what follows that he trusted this word of Christ. In one sense it is very remarkable. Until that moment he had been fiercely opposed to Christ and to the disciples; and suddenly he is challenged by the Risen Saviour. It is not a very intellectual challenge; and there must have been endless questions which were still unanswered in his mind. But the voice said 'I am Jesus', and he trusted Christ's word.

Faith means taking God at his word. It is so important to grasp this, so that your Christian life does not go up and down depending on feelings and experiences. It is Christ's faithfulness that ultimately counts. He really means what he says. Paul later gave Abraham as the supreme example of faith, and in Romans 4 he writes about Abraham: 'No distrust made him waver concerning the promise of God, but he grew strong in his faith as he gave glory to God, fully convinced that God was able to do what he had promised.' This is the essence of faith. Of course, a real faith in Christ will result in a transformation of your life. John, in his first letter, explains that some of the marks of the new life which Christ brings are a new joy, a new desire to please God, a new hatred of sin, a new love for Christians, a new peace in your heart, a new strength to overcome temptation, and a new reality in prayer. These will not all appear overnight, but there should be increasing evidence in your life of the reality of Christ's promise. Don't be worried if you have occasional doubts. Every Christian has them at some time or other, especially a few weeks after a decisive step of personal commitment to Christ. However, we can counter these doubts by claiming and trusting a promise of Christ.

He began to pray

God told Ananias to go to Saul of Tarsus, 'for behold, he is praying' (v 11). This was the first thing that Saul did after his meeting with Christ on that road. Of course, Saul had been a very religious man and prayer was nothing new to him. But now for the first time he was talking intimately to a God who had become real.

This pin-points one of the main essentials in a continuing relationship with Christ. All friendships and relationships must be developed or else they are in danger of fading away. Perhaps the greatest secret of all in the Christian life is to spend some time with Christ every day. Christ himself gave us the pattern to follow. In Mark 1:35 we read something about a day in the life of the Master: 'And in the morning, a great while before day, he rose

and went out to a lonely place, and there he prayed.'
Notice that the time was 'in the morning, a great while
before day'! This, for the majority of people, is by far the
most satisfactory time to be alone with God. Someone has
said that the two main essentials for the Christian life are
a Bible and an alarm clock. Certainly there is need for
firm discipline on this point, as you will never find it easy.
But if you develop the habit of getting up that much
earlier to spend time alone with Christ every day, you will
be tremendously grateful for this habit as the time goes
on. Notice also the place where Christ prayed: it was 'a
lonely place'. It is essential that you find somewhere that
you can be alone and undisturbed for an unhurried time
for Bible reading and prayer. Some system of Bible study
will be invaluable, and many people have found Scripture
Union Notes to be a good guide for such regular study.

It will also be a help if you can read the Bible and study
it with a Christian friend. You may well find certain
questions arising in your mind or certain problems which
seem difficult to solve, and developing a friendship with
another Christian so that you can share these questions
and problems together will prove of immense value to
you. Start reading good Christian books also. There are
many of these on the market, and no doubt a Christian
friend will give you some guidance on this point.

He was willing to be known
Immediately he was baptised (v18), and by this, apart
from other meanings of baptism, he was openly confessing
his faith in Jesus Christ. For Saul of Tarsus this was a
tremendous step. He really burnt his boats, and it certainly was not easy for him. However, in my experience,
the Christians who have gone on with Christ have always
been those who unashamedly have confessed their faith in
Christ to their unbelieving friends. The secret disciple has
a terrible struggle. But if you confess Christ openly to
other people, as the opportunity arises, you will find that
the reality of his presence will steadily increase.

He made friends with other Christians
It is worth seeing in this passage that this wasn't so easy

for Saul: 'And when he had come to Jerusalem he attempted to join the disciples; and they were all afraid of him, for they did not believe that he was a disciple' (v26). However, he persisted and soon he was thoroughly involved with other Christians. The New Testament knows nothing of the isolated Christian. Every person who committed his life to Christ automatically joined in with other Christians. They came from various backgrounds, had different personalities, and some of them found that their temperaments clashed. Nevertheless, to remain apart from Christian fellowship would have been to court disaster. Every Christian needs a live fellowship of true believers who know and love the Lord Jesus, who are studying his word, and seeking to serve him in the community. If you do not know of such a fellowship in your immediate area, do your utmost to seek one out. There will almost certainly be a group of such disciples somewhere, and you will find it of immense personal help if you throw in your lot with them.

He tried to tell others

'And in the synagogues immediately he proclaimed Jesus, saying, "He is the Son of God"' (v30). It is worth noticing that he went straight to the place where he was known. Certainly your prime responsibility for Christian witness will be amongst your friends and your circle of acquaintances. If you think of it, you have a unique responsibility here, because no one else in the whole world has the same circle of friends and acquaintances. What can you say to them? Well, once again, don't preach at them, but when the opportunity arises give a personal testimony of how you found Christ, and what he has come to mean to you. Also, as soon as possible, learn the basic steps towards a personal relationship with Christ, and learn a number of simple verses to guide a friend to the same relationship that you have found yourself. In the first half of this chapter I gave one way of explaining the steps to Christ; here is another way which I have found to be of great value over the years.

A Admit your need
The fact of sin – Romans 3:23; 1 John 3:4; Matthew 22:37

The consequences of sin – Romans 6:23; 1 John 1:5–6; Isaiah 59:1–2

B *Believe that Christ died for you*
Isaiah 53:5–6; 1 Peter 2:24; 3:18

C *Count the cost*
(1) Repentance – Isaiah 55:7
(2) Surrender – Mark 8:34   } or Mark 8:34–38
(3) Witness – Romans 10:9–10

D *Come to him*
John 1:12; Revelation 3:20
or Matthew 11:28; John 6:37

His life showed a difference

'And all who heard him were amazed, and said, "Is not this the man who made havoc in Jerusalem ...?"' (v21). Right from the start Saul impressed those who knew him by the marked difference that Christ had made in his life. This, of course, was one of the outstanding features of Christ himself: that although he mixed with every kind of person, he was always quite different. This was part of his immense attractiveness. People marvelled at his graciousness and love and compassion. A Christian is not called to obey hundreds of rules. He is called to walk with Jesus. Therefore, concerning any questionable activities or pursuits, the practical test is, can I really pray about this? Can I do this knowing that Christ is with me? The Bible, in fact, gives us three guides for all that we say and do:
(*a*) Will it help or hinder my Christian life? (see Hebrews 12:1)
(*b*) Will it help or hinder someone else's Christian life? (see 1 Corinthians 8)
(*c*) Is it to the glory of God? (see 1 Corinthians 10:31).

He was filled with the Holy Spirit

When Ananias came to Saul he laid his hands on him and said, 'Brother Saul, the Lord Jesus who appeared to you on the road by which you came, has sent me that you may regain your sight and be filled with the Holy Spirit' (v17). This was the key to the whole of his life and ministry. Without this he would have been empty, powerless, struggling to do what he felt was right but with no strength to accomplish it. The greatest need for each Christian is to learn what it is to be filled with the Holy Spirit, and to go on being filled with the Holy Spirit day by day. Jesus once made a promise, in Luke 11, to those who were conscious that they had 'nothing to set before' those in need. He said 'If you then, who are evil, know how to give good gifts to your children, how much more will the heavenly Father give the Holy Spirit to those who ask him!' (v13). If you long to know the fullness of God's power in your life, humbly claim this promise and pray that your Heavenly Father might fill you with the power of his Spirit that you might be able to witness to Jesus boldly and clearly. The Holy Spirit is the one who makes Jesus more real to you, and who will guide you and teach you from God's word as you study it daily. Let him possess and control your life day by day, and you will increasingly be able to say, with absolute conviction, *My God is real*.

In Search of God

DAVID WATSON

KINGSWAY PUBLICATIONS
EASTBOURNE

Contents

Introduction

Some years ago the BBC produced a programme on six major religions of the world, including Christianity. They looked for a title which would serve as a common denominator for all six religions. They called the programme *Man in search of God*.

This was a very fair description of man's search for spiritual reality, which is to be found all over the world, from pagan ritual to cathedral worship, from ouija board experiments to pentecostal fervour, from radical theology to biblical authority, from transcendental meditation to missionary zeal. In countless ways, we see this search for God, or at least for some kind of spiritual reality. Is there anything which transcends the material world of the five senses? Is there a power or person greater than ourselves that will lift us out of our meaningless existence to what is real and true?

And if there is no God, if God is dead, if there are no answers, what then? Many today realize the total futility of life unless there is some infinite reference point. Naturally, therefore, even in sophisticated scientific circles, we find man in search of God.

In some respects, this is not such a good title for the Christian faith. The prophets of the Old Testament, the apostles of the New, and supremely Jesus himself, were all insistent on one point: that God is in search of man. 'For the Son of man came to seek and save the lost,' said Jesus to one bewildered man, startled by the discovery that God had taken the initiative in the search. This is the Christian contention, that God has made, and always makes, the first move.

Nevertheless, we are not to be passive observers. And if the Christian revelation stresses God's initiative, it equally calls for our response. 'You will seek me and find me; when you seek me with all your heart, I will be found by you,' said God through the prophet Jeremiah. Jesus said the same thing, 'Seek, and you will find.' It would seem that the meeting-point occurs when God's search for man and man's search for God coincide.

This is what this book is all about. In our search for God, where do we start? What assurance can we have that there is a God to be found at all? Has he spoken to us? Has he shown himself? Where can we find him? How can we find him? How shall we know if and when we have found him? What relevance has all this for today?

The substance of these chapters has come from a number of university missions over a period of seven years: in particular Keele, Sussex, Manchester, Leicester, Aston, Oxford, Liverpool, Bangor and Birmingham, in England; and Christchurch, Dunedin, Massey and Auckland in New Zealand. Not only at these universities, but in many towns and cities in different parts of the world, it has been increasingly obvious to me that the vast majority of men, women and young people, from widely different backgrounds and cultures, are searching for God.

I am deeply grateful for all that I have learnt from those who have helped me on these missions, and from Christian students who have frequently shown me the reality of God in their own lives.

My gratitude, too, must be expressed to Miss Mary Pratt, my tireless and patient secretary, and to the publications department of the Church Pastoral Aid Society who have encouraged and guided me in the writing of this book.

1
Why Only Jesus?

No one can dispute the immense interest in the person of Jesus today. Admittedly the established churches are not heading the opinion polls for popularity; and queues form more quickly for 'eyes down at 7.30' in the bingo halls than for 'eyes up at 6.30' in the parish churches. Nevertheless the focus of attention all over the world has been swinging back to Jesus Christ.

The musicals *Godspell* and *Jesus Christ Superstar* have scored hits in the world of entertainment. Jesus festivals and Jesus marches have attracted tens of thousands. Jesus stickers and Jesus movements have left their mark on countless young people who have been far removed from conventional church-going. Christian Unions and Fellowships which centre unashamedly on the person of Jesus are often booming. Student missions in Oxford and Cambridge have seen an average of almost 1,000 students each night for eight nights in a row at the main meetings. The subject? *Jesus Christ Today, Christ Alive*. What other society, or what other theme, could draw such numbers?

The Bible, too, continues to be the world's best seller. For example, the complete Living Bible (a modern paraphrase) sold twelve million copies in two years, and has now passed beyond the twenty-eight million mark! This says nothing about the sales of the New Testament alone, or other sections of the Bible. And this is only one version! Why such astonishing popularity? Be-

9

cause the substance of the Bible is still utterly compelling; and the heart of that substance is Jesus Christ.

Every now and then you will find this advertisement in the national newspapers: 'Born in poverty. Lived only 33 years. Spent most of his life in obscurity. Never wrote a book. Never had any position in public life. Was crucified with two thieves. And yet, 2,000 years later, more than 950 million people follow him.' Although that figure no doubt includes many who are purely nominal Christians, the final comment from the advertisers seems justified: 'Surely it must be worthwhile to find out more about Christ.'

Why Jesus?

Why do we start with him? Why not God himself? Or why not go further back still and consider some of the philosophical questions that lie behind the whole assumption of God's existence?

When Paul visited Corinth, he found there two distinct groups in that multi-racial and permissive society; and the situation in this respect, at least, has changed very little in 2,000 years.

First, there were those who demanded tangible proof. 'If God is God,' they said, 'let him prove himself. Let him do something. Let him demonstrate to us his existence.'

The agnostic writer James Mitchell once wrote in *The God I Want* (Constable): 'The value of a god must be open to test. No god is worth preserving unless he is of some practical use in curing the ills which plague humanity – all the disease and pain and starvation, the little children born crippled or spastic or mentally defective: a creator god would be answerable to *us* for these things at the day of judgement – if he dared to turn up.' In other words, we want a satisfying sign, some tangible proof that God exists, especially in the meaningless muddle of the world today.

Secondly, Paul found those who were always asking questions: searching, seeking, discussing, debating, submitting all religious concepts to human reason. So it is today. 'First of all,' wrote Stephen Hopkinson also in *The God I Want*, 'I want a god who makes sense out of life as we know it, who gives meaning to the natural processes of the universe. Second, I want a god who makes sense of the existence of "me," the personality of which I am conscious in myself. . . .' I want a god I can understand, who fits in with my rational thought, and who answers some of my deepest questions.

What did Paul say to both those groups, the one requiring a sign, the other seeking after wisdom? 'We preach Christ crucified!' he said. This may be a stumbling block to some and stupid to others, but Christ in fact is both the wisdom and the power of God. Therefore if we want to understand God, we must start with Jesus. If we want to experience the power and reality of God, we must begin with Jesus.

Jesus himself once said exactly the same thing. His disciples were asking some basic questions: What is the way to God? What is God like? They were puzzled and confused, as many are today. Do you really want to know the way to God? asked Jesus: 'I am the way, I am the truth, I am the life; no one goes to the Father except by me.' (John 14:6 (TEV)) Do you really want to see God? 'Whoever has seen me has seen the Father.' (John 14:9 (TEV))

Of course, if there is an infinite personal God at all, then by definition he is infinitely greater than our total finite human understanding. Therefore we could not begin to understand him unless he had revealed himself to us. Man by wisdom cannot find God, said Paul, and this surely is obvious: the greatest philosophers in the world have discussed the question of God's existence for 3,000 years, with no answers to their questions at all! Most have now given up the search, and narrow the field to linguistic analysis instead!

God must therefore be known by revelation. He must 'speak' to us in ways which we can understand. Otherwise, no communication is possible. The urgent question therefore is this: Is there any word from God? Has he spoken to us?

The biblical answer is quite clear: 'In the past God spoke to our ancestors many times and in many ways through the prophets, but in these last days he has spoken to us through his Son.' (Hebrews 1 : 1f (TEV)) 'Before the world was created, the Word already existed, he was with God, and he was the same as God. . . . The Word became a human being and lived among us. We saw his glory, full of grace and truth. This was the glory which he received as the Father's only Son.' (John 1 : 1, 14 (TEV)) Devastating claims! Here is God communicating himself in the most meaningful way possible to human beings: not in a philosophy, nor in a metaphysical or ethical system; but 'the Word became a human being.' Here is something we can really understand. It communicates with people of all races of all generations, irrespective of culture, creed, education, environment. We are not discussing some 'eternal consciousness,' some 'impersonal life-force' or 'cosmic energy' (whatever those words mean). This is the most tangible self-revelation of God anyone could possibly ask for – the Word became a human being!

Martin Luther once said about Jesus: 'He ate, drank, slept, waked; was weary, sorrowful, rejoicing; he wept and he laughed; he knew hunger and thirst and sweat; he talked, he toiled, he prayed . . . so that there was no difference between him and other men, save only this, that he was God and had no sin.' Now the God who has revealed himself like that is someone whom we can understand. He communicates. Some got the message of Jesus so powerfully that they tried desperately to destroy him. They were unable to escape the challenge that God's Son conveyed. 'Show us the Father, and we shall be satisfied,' they cried. But there was no further answer needed when Jesus replied, 'Whoever has seen me has seen the Father.'

That is why we must start with the person of Jesus in our search for God. But –

Why only Jesus?
This is the stumbling-block of today: the uniqueness and exclusiveness of the claims of Christ – that he alone is the way to God and to heaven and to life. Believe in God himself, if you want to; seek after religious experiences, follow one guru or another – but why only Jesus?

> *Jesus Christ Superstar,*
> *Do you think you're what they say you are?*

Most people believe that the different religions of the world are like different paths up to a mountain, all leading to the same destination. Which one you take is of no great importance. Whether or not there is anything at the top of the mountain may be a matter for debate. But the common view is that Christianity is simply one of the great religions of the world, and that Christ is simply one of the great religious teachers – not the only.

Gandhi once said, 'The need of the moment is not one religion but mutual respect and tolerance of the different religions.... The soul of religions is one, but it is encased in a multitude of forms. Truth is the exclusive property of no single scripture.... I cannot ascribe exclusive divinity to Jesus. He is as divine as Krishna or Rama or Mohammed or Zoroaster.' (Quoted in *Christianity & Comparative Religion*, by J N D Anderson (Tyndale).)

A song by Quintessence says over and over again, 'Jesus, Buddha, Moses, Gauranga; Jesus, Buddha, Moses, Gauranga.' This is the spirit of the age. The all-embracing religion is Love. Although the Bible says 'God is Love,' most people today read that the other way round: 'Love is God.' Providing you love, that is God; and it does not matter at all what you believe or which religion you belong to. Therefore why only Jesus?

The position is considerably confused by the popularity of Eastern mysticism: Hare Krishna, transcendental meditation, occultism and spiritism, and from time to time the startling claims of a religious leader such as the guru Maharaj Ji, 'the Divine Light.' Let us look at this particular prophet more closely, as his photograph is appearing on hoardings and windows all over the world today.

The guru Maharaj Ji undoubtedly claims that he is the Christ for today. He accepts that Jesus, Mohammed, Krishna, Moses and others have been Divine Lights, or gurus, in the past; but they are all in the past and of the past, and everyone needs a perfect guru for today. According to the Maharaj Ji, his father had the True Knowledge of Divine Light, and now that same Knowledge and Light has been passed on to the son.

What are we to make of such claims? In the first place the Maharaj Ji quotes Jesus freely – and often inaccurately – and he is clearly trying to give the impression that he is saying now what Jesus said 2,000 years ago. If both are Divine Lights, this clearly must be so: 'The Knowledge itself has always been the same.' The trouble is that there are major and serious contradictions on most of the vital issues. For example, the Maharaj Ji says that God is not a person, but 'cosmic energy'; Jesus said that God is so personal that we are to think of him as 'our Father.' The Maharaj Ji says that there is no sin, only 'an active mind'; Jesus taught that sin was man's number one problem and indeed the basic cause of all the other problems in the world, a spiritual cancer that threatens to destroy us. The Maharaj Ji says that there is one atonement; Jesus declared that he came supremely 'to give his life as a ransom for many,' thereby taking away our sin and making reconciliation with God possible. The Maharaj Ji says that there is no resurrection; Jesus not only said that there is, not only claimed to be the resurrection and the life himself, but actually rose again from the dead to demonstrate the truth of his teaching. The Maharaj Ji says that there is no judgement; Jesus said that judgement is as certain as death, and much of his teaching was taken up with this solemn theme.

Whether or not you believe either teacher, it is quite impossible for *both* Jesus *and* the guru Maharaj Ji to possess the same divine knowledge and light, which is the guru's claim.

In the second place, and more simply, a high-caste Brahmin from India smiles at all the fuss made in the West concerning the Maharaj Ji. 'In my country of India,' he said, 'there is nothing so special about him at all. We have many of such people in India!' He is simply a much more intriguing figure for those of us living in the West. Yet even in the West we should not be deceived so easily. Periodically a prophet arises, making startling claims and promises, deceiving a few thousand followers. The Korean Sun Myong Moon is another example.

I am not in any way wishing to dispute the personal sincerity of these men. But religious history is studded with numerous individuals who in turn have claimed to be 'the Christ,' 'the guru,' 'the Divine Light' of that day; and Jesus himself warned us that 'false Christs and false prophets will arise, and show great signs and wonders, so as to lead astray, if possible, even the elect.' (Matthew 24: 24)

It is important to stress that Jesus did not say that all those of other faiths were wholly evil. Of course not! He recognized the love, beauty and truth that often did exist in those who were not his followers. Likewise, the Christian does not claim that he is always right and others always wrong, that he is always good and others always bad. Not at all! The light of God's truth has, in some measure, enlightened every man born into this world.

However, apart from certain general areas of agreement in the various religions and philosophies of the world, there are three absolutely crucial areas in which Jesus is unique.

For a note on the authenticity and historicity of the New Testament documents see the end of this chapter (pp 22-24).

1 The uniqueness of his person

'Jesus went to the territory near the town of Caesarea Philippi, where he asked his disciples, "Who do men say the Son of Man is?" "Some say John the Baptist," they answered. "Others say Elijah, while others say Jeremiah or some other prophet." ' (Matthew 16: 13–14 (TEV))

Today, virtually everyone would go as far as that: Jesus was one of the prophets, one of the great religious leaders of the world. I have never met anyone who has seriously disputed that. Though some would agree with Gandhi: Jesus is as divine as Krishna or Rama or Mohammed or Zoroaster – but no more. That is the one thing you cannot say about Jesus!

Suppose, for example, you were present when I was speaking at a gathering of people. What would your reaction be if I said something like this in my address: 'Do you want to know what God is like? If you have seen me, you have seen God. I and God are one. I am the way to God. No one comes to God except by me. I am the Truth. I am the Life. I am the Light of the World. I am the Resurrection and the Life; if you believe in me you will never die eternally. I have the authority to forgive sins. One day I am coming back to this world, and I will judge all people of all time. Your future destiny depends entirely on your personal response to me and to my words. If you believe in me you already have eternal life; but if you do not obey me you will not see life and the wrath of God will rest upon you.'

Further, supposing someone came up to me, knelt down before me, and, looking up in an attitude of worship, cried out, 'My Lord and my God!' Suppose that I not only accepted his worship, but I gently rebuked him for being so slow to believe.

Moreover, if I went on making such statements, not only at that gathering, but constantly and repeatedly for the best part of two years – what then? You are left with two logical alternatives. *Either* this is outrageous blasphemy from someone who is mad or bad or worse. Of course if you do not believe in God it is hardly 'blasphemy,' but at least it would be outrageous nonsense.

Or, these claims are true.

The one impossible conclusion is to say, 'This man is a good religious teacher!' No *good* religious teacher has ever made, or could ever make, the claims that Jesus incessantly made for himself.

Others said, 'That is the way . . .'; Jesus said 'I am the way.' Others said, 'That is the truth'; Jesus said 'I am the truth.' Others have pointed away from themselves to God; Jesus kept on saying, 'Come to me . . . Follow me . . . I and my Father are one . . .' Others said that they were messengers from God; Jesus said that he was himself the message. Indeed all that the prophets had spoken in the past was summed up in him. He was the Word made flesh, and that Word was God!

After the disciples had told Jesus that some were calling him 'one of the prophets,' Jesus went on to ask them, 'What about you? Who do *you* say I am?' At once Simon Peter came back with the answer, 'You are the Messiah, the Son of the living God.' Jesus was obviously overjoyed by his spiritual perception, 'Simon, son of John, you are happy indeed! For this truth did not come to you from any human being, but it was given to you directly by my Father in heaven.' (Matthew 16: 15–17 (TEV))

When Buddha was dying he was asked how people could best remember him. He urged his followers not to bother with that question. What mattered, he said, was his teaching and not his person. Christianity, however, is the only religion in the world which rests on the person of its Founder.

Of course anyone can make sweeping claims for himself; there is nothing very special about that. But if I, for example, made such claims, my life would show the falsity of them within five minutes. And even if I could deceive a few strangers for a short time, you ask those who know me best. You ask my wife! She could wax most eloquent on my faults and failings, and sometimes does! But look at Jesus. Ask his closest friends, who saw him tired, harassed, misunderstood and persecuted. Peter said, 'He was without blemish or spot.' John said, 'If we say we have no sin we deceive ourselves'; but of Jesus he said, 'In him there is no sin.'

Indeed, in Jesus you find a most perfect balance. He was sympathetic, but never weak; strong but never insensitive; loving but never indulgent; single-minded but never ruthless. Professor Anderson, in *Christianity the Witness of History* (IVP), once put it like this: 'He was a man not a woman, yet women as much as men find their perfect example in him. He was a Jew, not a European, African or Indian; yet men and women of every race find in him all they would most wish to be.'

Further, if Jesus was and is the Son of God, he alone has the right to speak on all the greatest issues affecting each one of us: life and death, God and man, man's need in the sight of God, the way in which we can find God.

You see, when it comes to these great questions, nobody knows the answer. Therefore whatever attitude anyone takes, it must be an attitude of faith. Ultimately it is faith either in Christ, or in your personal opinion that what Christ says is not true. Thus when you become a true Christian, it is not a sudden leap of faith from your personal opinion, with frankly all its uncertainty, to the person and authority and teaching of Jesus Christ.

It is certainly a great mistake to assume that the Christian has his head in the clouds, whilst the atheist or agnostic has his feet firmly on the ground. Concerning the great issues about life and death, we all have our head in the clouds, since no one knows. The Christian is simply calling to others to put their feet firmly on the rock of Jesus Christ. He alone is the one person worthy of our trust.

Moreover, everything about Christ endorses his

claims that he has the right or qualifications to speak on all these vital issues. If I have a pain in my chest, I may go to a friend who perhaps knows nothing about physical sickness. That friend might tell me that there is nothing really wrong, and I simply need to go to bed early, and all will be well tomorrow. However, I may go to a leading specialist, who warns me, after a series of very careful examinations, that I have a most serious disease and need an operation at once. Whatever advice I take, it is a matter of faith, but it is only sensible for me to put my trust in the one person who has the qualifications to speak. So it is with Jesus Christ.

Many people today feel no specific need of God; but Jesus came in part to tell us about our need, and to explain most forcibly that we all have the fatal disease of sin which needs urgent and immediate treatment if we are to experience the life and health that only God can bring.

This brings us to the second unique feature of Jesus.

2 *The uniqueness of his death*

Although death is inevitable for each one of us, the death of Jesus has the greatest possible significance.

It is worth noticing that the first thing that John the Baptist said when he saw Jesus was, 'Here is the Lamb of God who takes away the sin of the world.' (John 1 : 29 (TEV)) For centuries God had taught his people that sin really matters to him. Sin is as darkness, and God as light: darkness and light do not mix. Sin always separates us from God. Further, for centuries God had taught his people that because sin really matters, and because God is holy and can have nothing sinful in his presence, there can be no forgiveness without sacrifice, usually the shedding of the blood of an animal. Most often it was the blood of a lamb. Now when John the Baptist declared that Jesus was the Lamb of God who had come to take away the sin of the world, he was referring to the coming sacrifice of Jesus on the cross, when he would bear the full weight of our sin, thus making it possible for us to be forgiven and accepted by God.

Again the very first thing that Moses and Elijah discussed when they met with Jesus on the Mount of Transfiguration was 'his departure (= death), which he was to accomplish in Jerusalem.' The word 'accomplish' is an extraordinary word in the context. Who talks about accomplishing his death? But when Jesus on the cross cried out 'It is finished!' the word really means 'accomplished.' All that he had come to do, notably taking away the sin of the world, was now accomplished or completed or finished.

Again the very first thing that Jesus himself talked about when his disciples recognized him to be the Son of God was his coming death. 'From that time on Jesus began to say plainly to his disciples: "I must go to Jerusalem and suffer much from the elders, the chief priests, and the teachers of the Law. I will be put to death, and on the third day I will be raised to life." (Matthew 16:21 (TEV)) Constantly he taught his disciples about his approaching death. Elsewhere (Mark 10:45) he said that he had come into this world 'to give his life as a ransom for many.' A ransom is the price paid to set a person free. How can we be free to know God? How can we be free from the guilt of sin? How can we be free to face death without fear, and especially the judgement after death? There is no answer at all, apart from the death of Jesus Christ.

Some philosophies today try to solve the problem by saying that there is no sin, and no guilt, and that we are not responsible for our actions. However, those who shout most loudly about this are often those who shout most loudly about the rights and wrongs of society, and about the injustices in the world today. They show, by this, that they have a very deep understanding of responsibility, guilt and justice. He is far more concerned about this than we are. And there is no freedom from guilt, and no freedom from God's judgement apart from the death of Christ.

3 The uniqueness of his resurrection

Jesus told them that 'three days later he would be raised to life again.' And he was! Not only was the tomb empty, which even his strongest opponents had to admit; not only was the risen Christ seen by at least 550 people on eleven separate occasions over a period of six weeks; not only was the evidence so conclusive that it convinced the doubting, disbelieving disciples, and transformed Saul of Tarsus, the arch-enemy of the Christian Church; but the same risen, living Lord Jesus has convinced and transformed millions of people right up to the present day. Some of them have been atheists and sceptics, until they were honest enough to face the facts.

We shall look at some of these facts later in the book, but at the beginning of Matthew 16 there is an interesting confrontation between the Pharisees and Jesus.

They came to test Jesus's claim of being the Messiah by asking him to show them some great demonstration in the skies. He replied, 'When the sun is setting you say, "We are going to have fine weather, because the sky is red." And early in the morning you say, "It is going to rain, because the sky is red and dark." You can predict the weather by looking at the sky; but you cannot interpret the signs concerning these times! How evil and godless are the people of this day! You ask me for a miracle? No! The only miracle you will be given is the miracle of Jonah.' Then he walked away. (Matthew 16: 2–4 (TEV))

Here Jesus was calling their bluff. Some people are always protesting about lack of evidence, and demanding another sign. The truth is that there is abundant evidence for those who are willing to find Jesus. But very often those who do not believe do not *want* to believe. They do not want Jesus to interfere with their lives. All right, says Jesus, I won't interfere; but what will it profit you if you gain the whole world and lose your own life? Keep your world, if you want to; but you lose eternal life, and forgiveness, and God, and heaven, and everything of ultimate value!

One man, M Lepeaux, once founded a religion which was meant to improve on Christianity. Finding no very great success, he talked to his wise friend Talleyrand. 'There is one plan you might at least try,' said his friend. 'Why not be crucified and then rise again on the third day?'

Why only Jesus? Because no one else has claimed to be the Son of God and has justified his claims in every possible way. Because no one else has died for the sins of the world, making it possible for us to be absolutely forgiven. Because no one else has risen from the dead, no one else can give you any hope in the face of death, and no one else can offer you a living relationship with God himself. As Peter once said (Acts 4:12 (J B Phillips)), 'In no one else can salvation be found. For in all the world no other name has been given to men but this, and it is by this name that we must be saved.'

The heart of the Christian faith is a personal relationship with Jesus Christ. Christianity is neither a philosophy, nor a code of ethics, nor social action. It may involve all three, but the essence of it all is to know Jesus personally, and through him to enter into a wonderful relationship with God himself.

NOTE ON THE AUTHENTICITY AND HISTORICITY OF THE NEW TESTAMENT DOCUMENTS

The cumulative evidence for the reliability of the New Testament is powerful and weighty, and the person with serious doubts should study carefully *The New Testament Documents, Are They Reliable?* by Professor F F Bruce (IVP) – also, for more popular reading, *Runaway World* by Michael Green (IVP); *Ring of Truth* by J B Phillips (Hodder & Stoughton); *Christianity the Witness of History* by J N D Anderson (IVP). However, we should bear in mind the following points:

● We have about 5,000 Greek manuscripts in existence, some of which date back to the second century, or even late first century, AD. And amongst the differences in the manuscripts there is not a single dispute about any basic doctrine. Compare this with other ancient histories. The oldest manuscripts of the historian Tacitus comes 800 years after the original; and that of Thucydides, 1,300 years. Yet most scholars would accept these single manuscripts as reliable historical documents!

● Where historical details in the New Testament can be verified by other writings or archaeological discoveries, again and again they are found to be accurate. Dr Luke, for example, the author of the Gospel and the Acts of the Apostles, gives astonishing and painstaking details about all sorts of political, historical, geographical and nautical records, and their verification establishes him as a thoroughly accurate chronicler. There is no reason, therefore, to doubt other details which cannot be verified so easily.

● Although the first of the Gospels was written some thirty years after the death of Jesus, we must remember the following:

(*i*) The power of oral tradition was very strong – as it still is today in parts of the world where there is little or no access to written material.

(*ii*) Jesus taught in Aramaic, in a poetic style which is highly memorable, probably making his disciples learn his teaching by heart, as did most other Rabbis.

(*iii*) *Somebody* said those magnificent words, because we have them in black and white before us in our Bibles. And whoever said them was a genius.

(*iv*) There were many eye-witnesses alive when the first of the Gospels was written. Most disciples were passionately jealous of the truth about Jesus. There is no evidence that any disciples ever questioned the authenticity or accuracy of the Gospel records. No one tried to discredit them.

At the very least we should accept them as reliable historical documents, an authentic account of the life and teaching of Jesus of Nazareth.

2
Frustration, Apathy, Violence

Few things are more obvious in today's restless society than frustration. We see it in the mental illnesses which torment a growing number of the population, in the industrial tensions which are rife everywhere, in the deadlock in Northern Ireland, indeed almost everywhere you look. There is hardly a section in society, or a country in the world, free from frustration. In the musical *Hair* there is a song, which has as its constant refrain, 'Is there an answer? Tell me why, tell me why, tell me why . . .' The areas of frustration are well known.

First, there is *frustration about the future*. Fifty years ago, men boasted of the irresistible progress of mankind.

> Glory to Man in the highest,
> For Man is the master of things.

Utopia was around the corner. Today no one says anything so foolish. Most of the leading experts are extremely pessimistic. The computer scientist Professor J Forrestor of the Massachusetts Institute of Technology some time ago fed into the computers the relevant data of our time: population, pollution, capital investments, technology, natural resources, quality of life, and food production. Out came the prediction that civilization has perhaps one generation to survive. In many informed circles there is an atmosphere of total frustration. Man has no anwers. The Prophets of Doom today are not theologians but scientists.

The atomic bomb in Hiroshima in 1945 killed 87,000 people in one second. The hydrogen bomb, tested seven years later, was 1,000 times stronger. Only two years after that, American tests with the cobalt bomb proved that the destruction of all life on earth is possible.

The explosion of such a cobalt bomb would produce a radio-active cloud, whose degree of destruction would be 300,000 times stronger than the first hydrogen bomb, which in turn, was 1,000 times stronger than the first atomic bomb. Mankind has now sufficient nuclear explosives in the world to eliminate itself 50,000 times over. Indeed there is the equivalent of ten tons of TNT for every man, woman and child on this earth. Further, scientists are in the process of producing a biological bomb of devastating power. And in the history of mankind there never has yet been a weapon invented by man which has not been used, sooner or later.

Despite the 1974 Control of Pollution Act, our rivers are still being polluted. Hot water from power stations kills, while poisonous factory waste, sewage, coal washings, all take their toll of water creatures. And there is fear for the future of marine life too, when whales, seals and dolphins are slaughtered on a large scale. The oil pollution from wrecked tankers is horrifying, but on a minor scale compared with the possible dangers from oceanic transport of radioactive waste material for recycling.

The population explosion is yet another matter of extreme urgency. Within thirty years the population of the world will double. Yet already, more than 30,000,000 people die each year because they are too hungry to live. Arthur Koestler has said 'Human civilization is either on the verge of, or in the process of, exploding.'

A sixth-form girl, quoted in *Pornography, The Longford Report* (Coronet), expressed her dismay at world events like this:

If I were the sun
And I saw the things that people had done
I would eclipse myself
Forever.

Secondly there is *frustration about technology*. Clearly the build-up of nuclear weapons, the pollution of our environment, and the population bomb, are all directly caused by the astonishing 'progress' in science and technology. We build mindless machines, which then threaten our very existence. Charles Reich in *The Greening of America* (Allen Lane, The Penguin Press, 1971) talks about these mindless machines, or the progress of technology, in these words: 'They pulverise everything in their power: the landscape, the natural environment, history and tradition, the amenities and civilities, the privacy and spaciousness of life, beauty, the fragile, the slow growing social structures which bind us together. Organization and bureaucracy, which are applications of technology to social institutions, increasingly dictate how we shall live our lives, with the logic of organization taking precedence over any other value.' (© Charles A Reich, 1970; reprinted by permission of Penguin Books Ltd)

Moreover, the Professor of Psychology and Psychiatry in the University of Chicago, Dr Bruno Bettleheim, a man who once suffered in the concentration camps of Dachau and Buchenwald, says in *Encounter*, September 1969, that the frustration of today, which is so often outwardly expressed in terms of political or social issues is really the frustration that 'youth has no future.' 'Modern technology has made them obsolete. They have become socially irrelevant and, as persons, insignificant. Not because their future is bleak with a prospect of a nuclear holocaust, but because of their feeling that nobody needs them, that society can do nicely without them.... Their anxiety is not (as they claim) about an impending atomic war. It is not that society has no future. Their existential anxiety is that they have no future in a society that does not need them to

27

go on existing. It is modern technology – with its automation and computerisation – that seems to make man and his work obsolete, seems to rob him of his personal importance in the scheme of things.'

Thus the battle against the war machine is really the battle against the machine, because the machine, and all that goes with it in terms of bureaucracy and organization, tends to dominate human life. We are faced today with the same sort of frustration on a massive scale that some mill-workers felt in the nineteenth century when the machine threatened to destroy personal significance and the value of the individual. What is the meaning of man when trips to the moon have become almost commonplace and a third of the world is left starving?

Thirdly there is a *frustration about jobs and studies*. Many students, for example, have told me of the frustration that they feel about having to concentrate on some narrow, specialized area of academic study which seems totally unrelated to the huge and urgent problems of today. Therefore why bother? Why be pressurized into exams or degrees? Of what ultimate value is social status or financial reward? And even that is no longer guaranteed. Satisfying jobs seem increasingly hard to find. Strikes and redundancies are part of the daily scene.

A girl told me that she asked her humanist boyfriend, 'Why are you acting all the time? You never seem to be your real self.' He replied that if he stopped acting, life would become so meaningless that he could not live.

In the fourth place there is much *frustration with religion*. An increasing number today are searching for a spiritual solution to some of these problems, but, once again, many become frustrated and disillusioned. After all, the Church as a whole is not noted for its spiritual vitality. Although the organized structure of the Church has often been compared with scaffold surrounding a building, this scaffolding has apparently become so rusty that it cannot be moved and the existence of the living temple of the Church seems open to doubt. In *Waiting for Godot*, Samuel Becket says so much of the organized religion of our day 'seems as if God is dead and our lives have become an indefinite waiting for an explanation that never comes.'

'Oh God, if you exist at all, where are you? Why don't you answer me? Why are you so silent? My soul thirsts for God, for the living God.'...' And some, finding no reply, turn their backs on the Christian faith and become agnostics, atheists or humanists.

The curious thing is that even an atheist cannot get rid of spiritual hunger. A person might deny that food exists: but that will not stop him from being hungry physically. Equally a person might deny that God exists: but that will not prevent him from being hungry spiritually. Hence the frustration when religion does not seem to satisfy this basic spiritual hunger.

There are, of course, a host of other frustrations experienced today. Frustration with your job, your home, your marriage, your boyfriend or girlfriend, or indeed with yourself, which can be the most powerful frustration of all!

Now in the light of this world of frustration, there are two extremely common reactions. Most widespread of all is *apathy*. In *Future Shock*, Alvin Toffler (Pan): 'During World War II, a bearded Chindit soldier, fighting with General Wingate's forces behind the Japanese lines in Burma, actually fell asleep while a storm of machine-gun bullets splattered around him. Subsequent investigation revealed that this soldier was not merely reacting to physical fatigue from lack of sleep, but surrendering to a sense of overpowering apathy.' In other words, with his immediate situation so chaotic and alarming, his only protection from fear, panic or depression was total apathy. Who cares?

In the same book, Alvin Toffler talks about the bewildering change which is accelerating all the time. Many people, he says, cannot cope rationally with change, so they fall into 'drug-induced lassitude, video-induced stupor, alcoholic haze – when the old vegetate and die in loneliness.'

The main trouble with apathy, of course, is that nothing is solved, neither the problems nor the frustrations. We may repress our frustrations, and cover them up with an air of euphoria, and say that 'all is well.' However, the problems remain, and just beneath the surface the frustrations are very much there, often becoming one of the major causes of depression which is so prevalent today. Every year over 30,000,000 days are lost in industry in the UK alone due to depression and nervous disorder, far more than the total time lost in strikes. The National Health Service Bill for tranquillisers and pep pills runs at about £130,000,000 a year. Such figures are a small measure of the frustrations experienced in society today.

The second reaction to frustration is protest, which increasingly today is leading to *violence*. As the problems are so vast that improvements seem out of the question, many are saying that 'the only thing left is to bring down the whole system. With society so rotten, it can neither reform itself nor be reformed, but can only be born again through violent revolution.' (*Encounter*, September 1969) Jerry Rubin, the Yippie organiser, protested in *Encounter*, 'Who the hell wants to make it in America anymore? The American economy no longer needs young whites and blacks. We are waste material. We fulfil our destiny in life by rejecting a system which rejects us.'

The only trouble with violent protests and revolutions is not that they change too much, but that they change too little. They fail entirely to change the very nature of man, which ultimately is the cause of frustration. For example, the Czarist regime in Russia, corrupt and oppressive as it no doubt was and an immense cause of frustration among the workers, gave way to the Communist regime and to men like Stalin, who has been called the greatest mass murderer in human history. An Eastern European once made the shrewd comment that the only difference between capitalism and communism is that with capitalism man exploits man; and with communism the reverse is the case! Violence is nearly always a terribly frustrating answer to frustration.

Indeed the reason why both apathy and violence fail entirely to be a satisfactory answer is this. The basic frustration is with myself. This is where the real problem lies: in myself, in my heart, in my innermost being. My whole attitude towards society, towards both God and man, may be wrong. A student psychiatrist, who for many years had tried to help extremists and militants who were in difficulties, said this in *Encounter*, September 1969: 'Psychologically I find most student extremists hating themselves as intensely as they hate the establishment – a self-hatred they try to escape from by fighting any establishment.' Moreover, when the outward objective is reached, with university regulations changed or the end of a war, this often adds to the frustration. Because when the object of frustration is removed, the raw truth about frustration is seen as it really is: I am frustrated, not because of him, her, them or it, primarily, but because of *me*. I am the basic problem! And that is the thing which is so totally frustrating! An old saying puts it like this: 'The man who goes out to change society is an optimist. The man who goes out to change society without changing the individual is a lunatic!'

That is precisely why Jesus Christ is so utterly relevant for today. He comes to deal with the individual. He comes to change our heart and our nature. He is concerned with our attitudes first and foremost, not principally with our situation. And of course when our attitudes are changed, so often our situation is considerably changed as well. But even if the pressures and problems are exactly the same, Jesus is the One who can transform the whole scene by his living presence with us. In fact, Jesus alone has the answer to the most basic cries of modern man. What are these cries?

The cry for meaning

First, there is the *cry for meaning and purpose*. Of course there is nothing new about this: 3,000 years ago a preacher said, 'Emptiness, emptiness, emptiness, all is empty. What does man gain from all his labour and his toil here under the sun? To what purpose have I been wise? What is the profit of it? Even this is emptiness. So I came to hate life, since everything that was done here under the sun was a trouble to me; for all was emptiness and chasing the wind.' (Ecclesiastes 1 : 2f; 2 : 15, 17 (NEB))

However, this is thought to be the most poignant cry of today, and the root cause of most of our restlessness and frustration. According to Jean-Paul Sartre, 'Here we are, all of us, eating and drinking to preserve our precious existence, and ... there is nothing, absolutely no reason for existing.'

> *Life has no reason*
> *A struggling through the gloom;*
> *And the senseless end of it*
> *Is the insult of the tomb.*

I talked with an ex-heroin addict in Vancouver, who had suffered from heroin for three years but who had been wonderfully set free by Jesus Christ. He told me what I have so often been told, 'I took drugs because life was so completely futile and empty. I was searching for personal significance.' A university professor told me that an increasing number of mature men were coming to him depressed or in despair: 'Outwardly, it might be a case of job frustration; but inwardly they are all desperately searching for some ultimate meaning to life.'

Psychiatrists like Dr Victor Frankl of the University of Vienna call this the 'existential vacuum.' More and more people are coming into consulting rooms and clinics complaining of inner emptiness, a sense of total and ultimate meaninglessness of life. Dr Frankl has devised a 'logotherapy,' or existential analysis, to help patients to put meaning into their otherwise meaningless existence.

Jesus, knowing this basic need of man, kept on saying to people, 'Follow me! follow me! I am the light of the world. He who follows me shall not walk in darkness, but shall have the light of life.' A mother wrote to me a little time ago like this: 'I will never forget January 13th when you helped me to accept Christ as my Saviour and Lord. During those two weeks you made me understand where I was going. I was simply going through life like a blind person who didn't even want to see. Now it is wonderful to have a Friend so near me all the time.' Today she has found the glorious purpose and life that only Jesus can bring.

The cry for love

Secondly, there is the *cry for love*. Loneliness, as well as emptiness, is an acute problem for today. Part of the temporary popularity of the Beatles came from the huge relevance of such songs as Eleanor Rigby:

> *Ah, look at all the lonely people,*
> *Look at all the lonely people.*
> *Where do they all come from?*
> *Where do they all belong?*

So many people today want to be wanted, they long to belong. In a survey among students, 86% said that their main problem was loneliness. Most of us, if not all of us, will know this from time to time.

The reason is basic. The real and important world is the world inside us, not the world outside. In my outside world, I may know hundreds and thousands of people. There they are, all round me every day. Yet in my inside world, if there is no love, I shall be lonely. One young person, in desperate need, wrote to me about 'a great absence in my life – an empty silence within.'

However, Jesus offers a quality of love that will satisfy our inside world. The Spirit of Jesus can come to live within us, in our innermost being. God's love, wrote Paul, is poured into our hearts by the Holy Spirit. Jesus once talked to a woman was was trying to find satisfaction from sexual relationships. She had lived with six men, and still was lonely. Jesus answered: 'Whoever drinks this water will get thirsty again; but whoever drinks the water that I will give him will never be thirsty again. For the water that I will give him will become in him a spring which will provide him with living water, and give him eternal life.' (John 4: 13f. (TEV))

A university student who, until recently, was a cynical atheist wrote to me in this fashion, 'I had tried praying with no apparent effect – which to a very cynical atheist indeed is a pretty strong confirmation of why not to believe in a living God. And then came (a special service). I cannot describe what I felt or what I feel now, but I know that I have been privileged to realize and recognize what being forgiven and accepted by Jesus means. The wonder of it all amazes me, overwhelms me, and words fail to express the joy of realizing that I am never alone, never forgotten.'

Martin Niemuller, kept in concentration camps for many years, had only one possession, a Bible. He wrote: 'The Bible: what did this book mean to me during the long and weary years of solitary confinement, and then for the last four years at Dachau Cell-Building? The Word of God was simply everything to me – comfort and strength, guidance and hope, master of my days and companion of my nights, the Bread which kept me from starvation, and the Water of life which refreshed my soul. And even more: "solitary confinement" ceased to be solitary.'

Jesus alone can fully answer that cry for love. He loves us more than anyone could ever love us. He will never fail us, nor forsake us. Moreover, we belong not only to him, but to his family all over the world. He wants us to enter in to depths of relationships and love which come from God himself.

The cry for freedom

Thirdly, there is a *cry for freedom*. All too often today people blame their situation for their problems in life. 'If only we had a different government ... if only I had a different husband/wife ... if only something were different, all would be different.' But nearly always, it is not primarily our situation; it is our reaction to the situation that counts. The thing that really hurts is my pride, my jealousy, my resentment, my self-pity. These are the most frustrating things in life.

Jesus promised, 'If the Son makes you free, then you will be really free.' (John 8:36 (TEV)) God promised in the Old Testament, 'A new heart I will give you and a new spirit I will put within you; and I will take out of your flesh the heart of stone and give you a heart of flesh.' (Ezekiel 36:26) God wants to take away our stony, selfish, frustrated heart, and to give us instead a heart of love.

Recently I visited a prisoner called John, in one of Britain's top security prisons. John had a reputation of being one of the worst of the prisoners, consumed with bitterness and hatred for the police in particular and for society in general. He frequently made protests of one form or another. Sometimes he slashed his wrists. On one of these occasions, he thought he was dying, and in that moment of panic cried out to Jesus for help and forgiveness. At once Jesus came to set him free! God gave him a new heart and put a new spirit within him. I found John to be a most loving and gentle and peaceful prisoner when I saw him. It was a miracle! Later on he wrote to me this letter:

'This is my fifth time in prison and I am serving eight years for fraud.... I was dirty outside my body as I never used to wash. I was dirty inside my heart, lust, hatred, greed, revenge, anger and malice.... (Then he explained how he called out to Jesus for help.) All my pains, worries and burdens left me. I was able to stop smoking. I was able to stop reading dirty books. I was able to stop using dirty words; and the greatest of all I was able to love the people whom I had hated. I felt a completely different person, like being born again, and this is the great work of our Lord Jesus Christ. I was really cleaned inside out.... For the first time in my life, I am a free man – free of sin, free of the filth that has been inside me for years. The truth has made me free, the truth being the Lord Jesus Christ.'

Here is a man serving eight years in prison, and yet testifying that he is a 'free man.' Only Jesus could answer the deepest cry for freedom that is in the heart of man.

Take the case of Tom Skinner, one-time leader of a tough negro gang in New York, who was set free from his ways by the power of Christ. Shortly after his conversion, he was attacked quite unfairly by a white man. Tom Skinner records, 'I hit the ground, as he kicked me, shouting, "You dirty black nigger! I'll teach you a thing or two!" I got up and heard myself saying, "You know, because of Jesus Christ I love you." ' Here was a potentially violent man, and formerly a totally frustrated man, given the power to love his enemies. When we find Christ our situation may not immediately change, but our reactions, attitudes and habits can radically change. Only Jesus can do that.

The cry for forgiveness

Fourth, there is the *cry for forgiveness*. A student once described man's predicament to me like this: 'There is no one in the universe with the authority to forgive.' Indeed, this fact of guilt and the need of forgiveness, is extremely powerful and common, as it ought to be! We are all guilty in God's eyes; we have broken his laws and rebelled against him. And Jesus taught repeatedly that man's greatest problem was sin and his greatest need was forgiveness. Like the prodigal son (see Luke 15:11ff) we have all gone our way to lead our life as we want, and then find ourselves cut off from the only one who really loves and cares. Sin always separates us from God. There is a verse in the Bible which warns us that some of the consequences of sin will be 'confusion and frustration.'

I talked once to a girl who had a reputation in one university as being 'the toughest girl in our university.' She had slept freely around, and taken every known drug on the campus. Outwardly she did not care about anything and seemed quite hardened against the Christian faith. After a meeting she came up to me, cigarette dangling from her lower lip, to say that she had asked Christ into her life as her Saviour and Lord. My immediate thoughts were that time would tell. However, the next night she came to me again, and I hardly recognized her as being the same person. She told me about her first twenty-four hours as a Christian. She had spent most of that day crying. For years and years, she explained, in spite of her toughness and hardness, she felt 'as guilty as hell.' No one would have guessed it, but on that Sunday all her guilt had been coming out and she was overwhelmed by the love of Jesus. She could not really believe that he loved her, and died for her, and had taken away all her sins. It was wonderful for her to experience complete forgiveness. Another person wrote to me, 'I already feel a wonderful sense of freedom, as if a great weight has been taken off my shoulders.' God not only forgives, he forgets. 'Your sins and iniquities I will remember no more.'

The cry for hope
Fifth, there is a *cry for hope*. What hope has anyone in the face of death, apart from Jesus Christ? What hope can anyone give? What assurance could we possibly have, apart from Christ? But through the death and resurrection of Christ, with all the solid, historical evidence for that, there is a glorious answer to this cry for hope.

Jo was a lovely Christian girl, aged 20, but dying from leukemia. Three days before her death her father wrote to me this letter, 'All treatment for Jo has been stopped. Medically she has been given a few days only.

37

She knows the situation, is quite calm and is praying to Jesus....'

I heard from Jo's father again just after her funeral. 'Although so very weak and becoming more and more delirious, she died I know full of faith; and literally, but for the last few moments, held her right hand pointing up to Jesus as she could not speak.... In spite of all our sorrow it was wonderful seeing her coming closer and closer to Jesus.... We never forget that Jo is now with him and we would not want to disturb her happiness, even if we could.... Jo had a wonderful "funeral." The church was packed, and we all praised the Lord with hands raised.... "Bless the Lord O my soul, and let all that is within me bless his holy name."' Who else can give you hope in the face of death? There is no one apart from Jesus Christ.

The cry for God

Finally, there is a *cry for God*. In spite of the frustration with religion and much of the Church, many are still hungry for God or for some kind of spiritual reality. Jesus made it plain, 'Whoever has seen me has seen the Father ... I am the way, I am the truth, I am the life; no one goes to the Father except by me.' (John 14:9, 6 (TEV)) Therefore God becomes real only when we find Jesus and enter into a personal relationship with him. That is the heart of it all. It is not only God's answer to frustration; it is God's supreme purpose for our life; that we should know him and experience his love through a personal relationship with his son Jesus Christ. This is where we must start in our search for God.

3
Why is Man?

In the American University of Illinois, the College of
Fine and Applied Arts has tried to humanize today's
trend towards computerization. Each term the adminis-
tration sends out a card to check the student's programme. The accompanying letter begins something
like this: 'Dear 344-28-0430: We have a personal interest in you.'

Here we have the major personal crisis of today: not
'What is man?' but 'Why is man?' Has man any ultimate meaning or purpose at all? You see, the human
predicament is simply this. If there is no God then
there is no ultimate meaning to life at all. If God is
dead, man is dead. 'Man is a completely futile being'
– without God. This is what so many writers and philosophers and artists are saying today. I once asked a
well-known opera singer about some of the more avant-
garde music of today. 'Well,' she said, 'I am not too
keen on some of that. It is the music of man disturbed,
confused, restless – man who has lost meaning and
purpose because God is not real.'

If the primary question were 'What is man?' then,
of course, there are many answers which could be sum-
marized roughly in these well-known definitions. As to
his size, man is 'nothing but an accidental coincidence
on a minor speck of interstellar dust.' As to his ingre-
dients, man is 'nothing but fat enough for seven bars of
soap, iron enough for one medium-sized nail, sugar

39

enough to fill seven cups of tea, lime enough to white-wash one chicken coop, phosphorus enough to tip 2,200 matches, magnesium enough for one dose of salts, potash enough to explode one toy crane, and sulphur enough to rid one dog of fleas.'

As to his mechanism, he is 'nothing but complex bio-chemical mechanism powered by a combustion system which energizes computers with prodigious storage facilities for retaining encoded information.' As to his likeness man 'is nothing but a naked ape.'

The trouble with these 'nothing but' definitions is that, according to your own standpoint, once you have fully and accurately described man in terms of, say, 'a complex bio-chemical mechanism . . . ,' the impression is given that there is nothing more to be said. However, suppose you go into a beautiful village and take with you an architect, a painter, a poet, a historian, and an engineer, and ask each one to write a full and compre-hensive account of the village, you would have five very different reports. All would be equally valid, all complementing one another. No one could say that the village was 'nothing but' their particular description. And you tell the TV audience that Miss World is 'noth-ing but a complex bio-chemical mechanism,' and I think most of them will disagree. Or, if you like, put a beautiful computer in the place of Miss World, and see if you get the same viewing audience!

However, there are many like the humanist Dr Edmund Leach who reject any thought of man as a special creation by God, and say that 'there is no sharp break of continuity between what is human and what is mechanical.'

Now, if that were true, and if there were no ultimate meaning to life, then why bother about anything at all? For example, why get worked up about justice? Why protest about social or racial questions? How could I be fair or unfair, just or unjust, to what is basically a machine? If man were only a machine, determined bio-logically or psychologically, then why be concerned

about any political, social, racial or legal issue at all?
If man were less than a created being, frankly anything
goes.

> *She was beautifully delicately made,*
> *So still, so unafraid,*
> *Till the bomb came,*
> *Bombs are the same,*
> *Beautifully, delicately made.*
>
> C S Lewis

What is the difference between 'she' and 'it'? If man
were simply a cog in a vast soul-less machine, the individual would be completely expendable: he or she
would be a means to an end, an object to be used. It
is, of course, a common philosophy of today, shared in
particular by Marxists, nihilists, and the pushers of
pornography. (*Nihilism* is a philosophy of total scepticism. There is no meaning, no aim, no values, no purpose, no answer to the question Why?) If Marx's dictum
were true, that 'the material world to which we belong
is the only reality,' then anything goes. Dr Viktor
Frankl, who survived the Auschwitz concentration
camp, says that the nihilistic philosophies of the nineteenth century led to the death camps of the twentieth
century, and that even now there is a 'nihilist tendency
to devalue and depreciate that which is human in man.'
Whether for sex or violence, men and women often
tragically use one another. In an 'exclusive' interview
with a well-known national paper, Raquel Welch is re-
ported to have said, 'I am just a piece of meat ... I
fulfil the ambitions of other people to make money out
of me.' The article was called, 'The Torment of the
World's Number One Sex Symbol.'

Carrying this philosophy to its logical extremes, you
could do what you like with a slab of meat or with a
human machine. And for that matter, other human
machines could do what they like with you! Nothing
is fair or unfair. There is no justice, there are no rights
or wrongs, there are no safeguards of any kind, if man
is simply a machine. Some existentialist thinkers are

saying that it is as meaningful to run down an old woman in your car as it is to give her a lift! *Existentialism* is a philosophy of blind faith in personal experience. The existentialist goes from the dread of a meaningless existence to the brink of despair; and, having faced the situation, makes a deliberate commitment to a course of action. There are no absolutes: 'if it's true for *me*, it's true!' It therefore becomes a philosophy of total self-interest. It is important to see the logical implications of such a philosophy. All human values, personal considerations, love, caring, sharing, compassion, justice, honesty and friendship vanish if man is fundamentally a machine.

Practically speaking, of course, it is quite impossible to live consistently with this philosophy. We assume meaning in almost everything we do. We do have friends, we make love, we care about justice and injustice. We would not tolerate old women being run over with gay existentialist abandon! We do protest about many things. We make value-judgements about one another. We are not indifferent about Hitler's massacre of six million Jews or Stalin's murder of 20,000,000 people. And if we really believed in complete determinism all those values would be meaningless. Indeed most of our time we live, love, think and act so unlike a mere machine that you find Sartre, for example, saying, 'Man is absurd, but he must grimly act as if he were not!'

Why is man? The answer in the first place is to see him in the light of a Creator God. It is important to understand that if there is an infinite personal God at all, he must be infinitely greater than man's total understanding. Therefore we can know God only if he reveals himself to us, and breaks into our circle of understanding. And the Christian contention is that there is such a God, that he has revealed himself to us in a great variety of ways, one of which is creation itself.

Professor Tony Holland, Professor of Chemical Engineering in the University of Salford, was a scientific humanist up to the age of about 30. Then, in his own words, 'The first question I asked was "Is there a God?" On consideration, it was inconceivable to me that the complex system of which we are a part could have occurred without a Creator. Just as a great symphony testifies to the skill of the composer, the world and the universe testify to the wisdom and power of God. Science is but a description of God's work.'

Professor Edwin Carlstin, Biologist at Princeton University, has said 'The probability of life originating from accident is comparable to the probability of the Unabridged Dictionary resulting from an explosion in a printing factory.' Certainly the complexity, beauty, exquisite design, and purposefulness of creation points directly towards a Creator and Designer. Not that creation is any *proof* of God's existence, but at least it is a pointer. Of course there is much clearer evidence in the person of Jesus Christ, God's supreme revelation of himself: 'The Word became a human being.' Now in the light of a Creator God, several facts become clear.

The smallness of man

At times it is important to remember just how small we are. Franklin D Roosevelt used to have a little ritual with the famous naturalist, William Beebe. After an evening's chat the two men would go outside and look into the night sky. Gazing into the stars, they would find the lower left-hand corner of the great square of Pegasus. One of them would recite these words, as part of their ritual: 'This is the spiral galaxy of Andromeda. It is as large as our Milky Way. It is one of a hundred million galaxies. It is 750,000 light-years away. It consists of 100 billion suns, each larger than our sun.' They would then pause, and Roosevelt would finally say, 'Now I think we feel small enough. Let us go to bed!'

King David, gazing up into the heavens and seeing the night sky studded with stars, once exclaimed, 'Oh Lord, our Lord, how majestic is thy name in all the earth ...! When I look at thy heavens, the work of thy

fingers, the moon and the stars which thou hast established; what is man that thou art mindful of him, and
the son of man that thou dost care for him? (Psalm 8: 1,
3–4) The Bible speaks about man as having been
created from the dust: 'You are dust, and to dust you
shall return.'

It is necessary for us at times to be cut down to size.
There is in some circles today an arrogance in thinking about God, as though the basic question were, 'Why
should I bother with God?' The real question is, of
course, 'Why should God bother with me?' That is a
much harder question to answer. 'What is man that
thou are mindful of him?' In the words of the prophet
Isaiah, 'Behold, the nations are like a drop from a
bucket, and are accounted as the dust on the scales;
behold he takes up the isles like fine dust... All the
nations are as nothing before him, they are counted
by him as less than nothing and emptiness. To whom
then will you liken God, or what likeness compare with
him? ... Have you not known? Have you not heard?
The Lord is the everlasting God, the Creator of the
ends of the earth. ' (Isaiah 40: 15, 17f, 28)

Some people assume that we have a right to God's
love. They see man at the centre of the universe; and
God, if he exists at all, is simply there to give us our
rights and to meet all our needs. And providing God
is able to satisfy my ideas about him, and my ideas
about life, justice or love, then I might perhaps consider believing in him, as though I were doing him a
favour. What some fail to realize completely is that
God is at the centre of the universe. The question is
not 'Is God relevant to me?' but 'Am I relevant to
God?' How can *we*, tiny sinful, rebellious human beings, have any contact with an infinite, personal God
who is utterly holy? When it comes to man's rights before God, the only thing that we can say is that we have
the right to be judged. Many times it says in the Bible
'God resists the proud'; and if we come with all our intellectual guns firing away with arrogant arguments, we

shall never, never find God.

However, since there is a Creator God who has made man in his own image, we have another important fact.

The significance of man

Each individual, rebellious and sinful though he may be, is of tremendous significance in the sight of a Creator God. Being made in the image of God, man has at least five characteristics which are not shared by the rest of the animal creation. Man can reason, with powers of reflection; choose, as a free agent; love, consciously preferring one before another; and above all worship God and know God, and he is personally responsible to his Creator. He is meant to live in complete dependence upon God. Indeed the whole point of the Genesis 1 account of creation is that man is seen, not as the ape, but as the apex of creation. Some people get worried about the six days of creation. But quite apart from the fact that 'day' in Hebrew thought is simply a period of time, the main point, I believe, is that man is so much the crown of creation that the rest of the creation of the universe is as five days in comparison!

Further, God has made man with a large spiritual appetite which cannot be satisfied with anything less than himself. Few things are more obvious today than the profound spiritual hunger which exists everywhere. No one is like man! Man is unique in creation! After David cries out in his psalm, 'What is man that thou art mindful of him?' he goes on to say 'Yet thou hast made him little less than God, and dost crown him with glory and honour. Thou hast given him dominion over the works of thy hands; thou has put all things under his feet ... O Lord, our Lord, how majestic is thy name in all the earth!' (Psalm 8: 5–6, 9)

That is why it is wrong to use one another, to kill, to neglect, or exploit one another. Each individual human being has been made in God's own image. There is no philosophy in the world that gives such dignity and significance to man as the Christian faith. Indeed it is precisely because of this that Christians have always been in the forefront of social justice. It is Christians who have freed the slaves, emancipated women, cared for the sick, instituted Trades Unions, and brought education, medicine and justice to oppressed people all over the world. Of course Christians have made countless mistakes, and 'religion,' as opposed to the real thing, can be appallingly cruel and heartless. But wherever individual Christians and groups of Christians experience the love of God, this love will inevitably spill out in compassion towards the numerous needs of man.

However, it is because of the enormous significance of the individual in the sight of God, that we must also consider a third factor.

The sinfulness of man

Jesus taught repeatedly that the evils of this world can all ultimately be traced back to the fall of man, to the sinful nature of our hearts. In Ephesians 2 : 1 Paul reminds the Christians at Ephesus about their true spiritual condition, before God made them alive in Christ: 'You were dead through the trespasses and sins.' It is not that *God* is dead, as some are thinking and saying today; but that spiritually *we* are dead to God, which is a very different matter. Because of 'trespasses and sins' we do not naturally enjoy the living relationship with God; he is not real in our experience.

There are two main characteristics of a dead person, whether thinking physically or spiritually. First he is *helpless*. After all, what can a dead body do? Nothing except rot! Likewise a spiritually dead person is helpless to do the things he ought to do because, says Paul, he follows or is controlled by three things.

In the first place, he follows the course of this world: 'You drifted along on the stream of this world's ideas of living' (J B Phillips translation). Most people drift with the crowd, as a dead piece of wood floats down the river. How easily we are governed by the world around us! Keeping up with our neighbours, or with our particular social set or group is a very powerful principle. Various people tell me how they cheat the Income Tax Authorities, or fool around in ways that are illegal or immoral, but quickly add the rejoinder, 'Well, everybody does it!' The subtlety is this: we think that we can play with the world as we like. No, says Paul, the stream of this world is carrying you along. Elsewhere he says 'The world is trying to squeeze you into its own mould.' (Romans 12 : 2 (J B Phillips)) And it is frankly a mouldy mould, because it will take you right away from the living God. However, the spiritually dead person is helpless to prevent this.

In the second place, says Paul, the spiritually dead person follows the prince of the power of the air. We shall look at this more closely in a later chapter, but the New Testament teaches clearly that the whole world lies under the control of Satan whenever or wherever Christ is not personally accepted as King: 'The whole world is under the rule of the Evil One'. (1 John 5 : 19 (TEV) Satan is called 'the god of this world.' (2 Corinthians 4 : 4) We see this, of course, in all forms of occult practices, which are very much on the increase, but we also see Satan's activity in every part of life which seeks to draw people away from God's Son Jesus Christ: materialism, greed, and even entertainment or sport. A major Gallup poll over Western Europe, from 10,000 interviews, came to six conclusions:

- Religious beliefs are declining

- Morals have also slumped

- Honesty is on the wane

- Happiness is becoming increasingly hard to find

- Peace of mind is rare

- Hardly anybody believes in the devil: 'the devil has had it.'

However, it is quite clear that Jesus believed in a personal devil, and warned groups of people that they were under his control: 'You are the children of your father, the devil.' (John 8: 44 (TEV)) Naturally the spiritually dead person is controlled by the prince of the power of the air, and is helpless to do anything about it.

In the third place, the spiritually dead person follows the desires of body and mind, or the passions of the flesh. In the New Testament 'flesh' refers to our self-life: selfishness, self-centredness, self-seeking, and all manifestations of self. William Temple once explained that this is the fundamental meaning of sin; 'I am the centre of the world I see: where the horizon is, depends on where I stand.... Education may make my self-centredness less disastrous by widening my horizon of interests: so far it is like climbing a tower, which widens the horizon for physical vision, while leaving me still the centre and standard of reference.' Once again the spiritually dead person is helpless to do anything about this.

The second mark of a dead person is that he is *separated* from other people. In physical death this separation is obvious and the cause of sadness and bereavement. But spiritual death is even more serious. It not only brings separation between man and man, hence all the tensions and problems in society; it brings a separation between man and God. Paul wrote to the Ephesian Christians, 'Remember that you were at that time (before your conversion) separated from Christ, alienated from the commonwealth of Israel, and strangers to the covenants of promise, having no hope and without God in the world.' (Ephesians 2: 12) Here he uses five words or phrases to express this estrangement: separated, alienated, strangers, no hope, without God. Further this separation from God now, which we naturally feel, unless we do something about it now, will one day become a full, final and eternal separation from God and from all good. This is what Christ called 'outer darkness,' 'a great gulf fixed,' 'hell.' Perhaps the most disturbing feature about this is its absolute fairness. The essence of judgement is that God gives us what we ourselves have chosen. If I want to be on my own, on my own I shall be. If I do not want God to interfere with my life, God will not interfere; he leaves me utterly alone, and that is the essence of hell.

If the story stopped at this point, the situation would be fairly desperate: by nature we are all spiritually dead, helpless and separated from God. Of course, since we have all gone our own way and turned our backs on God, and since we have frequently disobeyed him and broken his laws, we unquestionably deserve his judgement.

Fortunately that is not the end of the matter. '*But God*,' wrote Paul in two tremendous, triumphant words, 'But God, who is rich in mercy, out of the great love with which he loved us, even when we were dead through our trespasses, made us alive together with Christ (by grace you have been saved).' (Ephesians 2 : 4f) Entirely through God's love and mercy he offers us in Jesus Christ three things.

First, we need no longer be spiritually dead but can become alive in Christ. The living God, the Creator of all that exists, can become a reality in our own personal experience. We can know God as a Father, we can experience Jesus as our Friend. A journalist said to me in a letter, 'It is really wonderful to feel alive with Christ.'

Secondly, we need no longer be separated from God, but personally related with him in a glorious intimate relationship that not even death can destroy. And this reconciliation has been made possible for one reason only: by the death of Jesus Christ. 'But now, in union with Christ Jesus, you who used to be far away have been brought near by the death of Christ.' (Ephesians 2 : 13 (TEV)) Christ has become our Mediator, perfectly representing both parties, God and man, and has borne the full weight of our sin in order to bring us back to God.

Thirdly, we need no longer be helpless, but now able to fulfil God's special purpose for us in this world. As soon as a person commits his life to Jesus Christ, the Spirit of God comes to indwell his whole being. In the first chapter of his letter to the Ephesians, Paul prayed that the Christians might understand that the power within them in the person of the Holy Spirit is the very power that raised Jesus from the dead. Paul once despaired of the impossibly high standards that God had set before him: 'For even though the desire to do good is in me, I am not able to do it. I don't do the good I want to; instead, I do the evil that I do not want to do.... What an unhappy man I am!' What is the answer to this human predicament? 'Thanks be to God, through our Lord Jesus Christ! ... For the law of the Spirit, which brings us life in union with Christ Jesus, has set me free from the law of sin and death.' (Romans 7: 18f, 24f; 8: 2 (TEV) – see Chapter 7 in this book for a fuller discussion of this point.) With the Spirit of God within us, the individual is able to fulfil his God-given role, which would otherwise be totally impossible for him. 'If anyone is in Christ, he is a new person altogether.' Exactly how this process starts we shall examine more closely later in this book.

4
Suffering, Hell and a God of Love

A God of love? As soon as anyone begins to speak about the existence of a loving, heavenly Father, two huge problems are raised: the suffering of man, and the judgement of God. If there were no loving God, then of course there would not be problems. This is the reason why some of the other religions have no great difficulties with the question of suffering: they do not accept the concept of a loving God.

It is important, however, to see the logical implications of all this. If there were no God of love, then there would be no justice in the universe, no fairness, no ultimate control. Anything would go! The world would be in chaos, one grotesque meaningless muddle. If I shut my eyes to an infinite personal loving God, of course I am left with darkness, a hopeless situation and a meaningless existence. The early Christians knew only too well that if they closed their eyes to the existence of God, to life after death, to the resurrection of Christ. to heaven and hell, to the justice of God and the vindication of right over wrong, then the world would become one big horrid mess: 'If our hope in Christ is good for this life only, and no more, then we deserve more pity than anyone else in all the world.' (1 Corinthians 15: 19 (TEV))

On the other hand, if we accept the existence of a loving God, then how can we reconcile this with the exceedingly ugly fact of suffering? How can we account for Christ's teaching on judgement and hell? In *The God I Want*, William Miller asks, 'To what divine purpose and in what loving brain was a scorpion forged? What holy chastening is intended when babies are born deformed in mind or body? Is it God's will that two-thirds of the world's population are undernourished? ... Any hospital will show a gallery of pain which is almost unbearable to the viewers. ... If there is a God, he is responsible.'

Two truths must be borne in mind from the start. In the first place, there is certainly no slick answer to the problem of suffering. Anyone who has witnessed the horrifying scenes of starvation, or cared for those suffering from cancer, leukemia, multiple sclerosis, or mental torment, will not be glib with a few pious clichés. Most of us will be faced with the huge unanswerable question 'Why?' all too often.

In the second place, however, we have to admit that a great deal of suffering is caused directly by ourselves. 'Where do all the fights and quarrels among you come from? They come from your passions, which are constantly fighting within your bodies. You want things, but you cannot have them, so you are ready to kill; you covet things, but you cannot get them, so you quarrel and fight.' (James 4: 1f (TEV)) In the vast majority of cases we need to look no further for the cause of suffering than the greed, lust, pride, jealousy, resentment, and selfishness that is in the heart of man. As C S Lewis wrote in *The Problem of Pain* (Fontana), 'It is men, not God, who have produced racks, whips, prisons, slavery, guns, bayonets and bombs; it is by human avarice or human stupidity ... that we have poverty and overwork. But there remains, nonetheless, much suffering which cannot thus be traced to ourselves. Even if all suffering were man-made, we should like to know the reason for the enormous permission to torture their fellows which God gives to the worst of men.' This is the dilemma which we cannot escape. What, then, can we say about suffering?

1   Our whole approach must be right

If God is God, we could never understand all his ways and works. If we could, God would be no bigger than our minds, and therefore not worth believing in. To say, 'I do not know why there is all this suffering' does not mean that there is no reason; but that, as a tiny human being, there is a limit to my understanding; which is true on countless issues. It would be arrogant to say, 'Because I do not know of any reason, therefore there is no reason.'

This, of course, is the message that comes so powerfully through the book of Job. God does not have to justify his existence to us. And if I say to God, 'You first give me satisfactory answers to my questions before I am prepared to consider believing in you,' my whole attitude is fundamentally wrong. Several times in the Scriptures we are told that 'God opposes the proud, but gives grace to the humble.' (James 4:6; 1 Peter 5:5, Psalm 138:6) Until, then, I am prepared to humble myself before God, he has nothing for me at all! Our whole attitude therefore must be one of humble honest enquiry.

2   Suffering is ultimately due to man's rebellion against God, although on many occasions we may not be able to trace the direct links.

We have already seen that often we can; but what about earthquakes, floods, and tornadoes? Surely we must blame God for these? I do not know of any simple answer to this problem, although today, of course, man is hardly in a position to blame the God of the environment, when man's pollution is so appalling on every side. However, the Bible certainly implies that creation itself is corrupted and polluted; and this is directly or indirectly due to the corruption and pollution of man. Since man was given the responsibility of looking after God's world, when man fell, creation fell. It is simply avoiding our own responsibility and guilt if we choose God as a convenient scapegoat.

3   It is frequently true that it is not so much our situation but the way that we react to it that counts.

A little time ago I talked with two young fathers within a period of about four months. Both had tragically lost their children of four or five. One had died of leukemia; the other had been drowned in a swimming pool. One father had been a professing Christian but was now, through the experience, a militant atheist. The other father had been a humanist and was now, through the experience, almost a Christian. Here were two very similar tragic experiences but with totally different reactions to each situation.

These reactions are tremendously important. If I become bitter and resentful in my suffering, I still have my suffiering, but on top of that I have to contend with my bitterness and resentment as well; and this may be even worse than any initial suffering. Certainly it would be worse for other people, and I am responsible for that.

On the other hand, if in my suffering I open my heart to the love and peace and friendship of Jesus Christ, then this will wonderfully transform the entire situation – a fact which I see in pastoral work virtually every week of my life.

4   Those who know more of the love of God in their experience than anyone I have ever met, also have known more suffering than anyone I have ever met.

This may be a curious fact, but suffering can produce great depth of character, understanding and spiritual experience, providing we react to it in the right way. Suffering is not always one total disaster.

Richard Wurmbrand, the Rumanian pastor who spent 14 years in a communist prison, including three years in solitary confinement, was able later to say this, 'We prisoners have experienced the power of God, the love of God which made us leap with joy. Prison has proved that love is as strong as death. We have conquered through Christ. Officers with rubber truncheons

54

came to interrogate us; we interrogated them, and they became Christians. Other prisoners had been converted. ... The Communists believe that happiness comes from material satisfaction; but alone in my cell, cold, hungry and in rags, I danced for joy every night.... Sometimes I was so filled with joy that I felt I would burst if I did not give it expression.... I had discovered a beauty in Christ which I had not known before.' (*In God's Underground* (W H Allen))

5   *It is often through suffering that God speaks.*
Naturally we all tend to be independent and self-sufficient. Therefore sometimes it is only through suffering that we begin to see our frailty and start asking the really important questions in life, particularly concerning the purpose of our existence and our relationship with God. Indeed, many of our problems come when we put ourselves at the centre of our universe; and God, if he exists at all, is simply around somewhere to fulfil a job.

All too often we assume that his job is to answer our needs, to give us our rights, and to make sure that everyone has a fair deal. Do you see what we are doing? We are treating God as our servant! Providing he does his job well, we are pleased; but if he should fail to serve me or one of my fellow men in a way that I think is right, then he is in trouble! We start to criticize him and blame him for his failures. And the common attitude towards God is to keep him standing outside the door, until perhaps we make a mess of things, then we decide to call him in to clear up the mess, only to send him out again.

What we so often fail to realize is that we are not at the centre of the universe: God is! God does not exist for the sake of man, but man exists for the sake of God. 'For you created all things, and by your will they were given existence and life.' (Revelation 4: 11 (TEV))

Further, if we start talking about rights, the only right we have is to be judged by him. We have been created by him, yet have rebelled against him. Therefor the primary question is not 'How can God allow suffering?' but 'How can God allow sinners into his presence at all?' How is it possible for us to experience his love and forgiveness and peace at all? How is it possible that an infinite holy God should be concerned with us at all? Those are the really difficult questions and it is sometimes through suffering that we begin to think deeply about these vital issues that affect every one of us.

6 *Jesus warned us again and again not to build our hopes and happiness on this world.*
Now in this world it is possible to experience a quality of life in Jesus Christ which is so rich and satisfying that the New Testament writers had to speak in superlatives.

We read there of a fullness of life, a love which surpasses knowledge, a peace which passes all understanding, inexpressible joy. Such phrases imply that no words can sufficiently describe the results of a rich relationship with God. Yet the New Testament writers knew, often in their own painful personal experience, that we are still very much living in a world full of suffering.

Unlike the prophets of Utopia, Jesus said that 'nation will rise against nation, and kingdom against kingdom, and there will be famines and earthquakes in various places: all this is but the beginning of the sufferings.' (Matthew 24: 7f) And one day, of course, we stand to lose everything that is of this world; so that it is our eternal relationship with God that is of ultimate importance.

The disciples once came to Jesus and asked him about the whole question of 'innocent suffering.' Two thousand Jews had been crucified by the Romans in Galilee; a tower had fallen and had killed eighteen people. 'Why does God allow it?' was their obvious question. Jesus did not tackle the philosophical question of suffering, but brought the matter straight back to a practical challenge. 'Do you think that these Galileans were worse sinners than all the other Galileans, because they suffered thus? I tell you, no; but unless you repent you will all likewise perish. Or those eighteen upon whom the tower in Siloam fell and killed them, do you think that they were worse offenders than all the others that dwelt in Jerusalem? I tell you no; but unless you repent you will all likewise perish.' (Luke 13: 2–5)

God therefore sometimes allows disasters to happen, partly to bring us to our senses. If we all knew that we had 70 years of life, we should be unbearably selfish and self-centred for 69 years 364 days, and then we would conveniently repent and expect to sail into heaven! But the point is that we do not know about tomorrow. Life is desperately uncertain and sometimes extremely short. We may have to meet our Creator and Judge at any moment. Therefore God, in his love, warns us. He speaks to us through his word and in our conscience. Sometimes he has to speak more loudly through suffering, whether ours or someone else's.

Now you may feel that it is a very poor thing if we turn to God only when we are crying out for help or when we are afraid of the judgement to come. So it is! It is a very poor thing indeed if we turn to him as a last resort, like clutching at a straw. But it is part of what C S Lewis calls 'the divine humility' that God is willing to accept us even on those terms. 'If God were proud, he would hardly have us on such terms; but he is not proud, he stoops to conquer, he will have us even though we have shown that we prefer everything else to him, and come to him because there is "nothing better" now to be had. The same humility is shown by all those Divine appeals to our fears which trouble high-minded readers of Scripture. It is hardly complimentary to God that we should choose him as an alternative to hell; yet even this he accepts. The creature's illusion of self-sufficiency must, for the creature's sake, be shattered.' (*The Problem of Pain* (Fontana))

The judgement of God

If God is a God of love, how can there possibly be a future judgement and hell?

In one sense it is hard to understand why some people get so upset by the concept of judgement. The necessity of judgement or accountability is built into our whole framework of life. All of us have to give an account of our time, work, money, or abilities to someone sometime. What is so strange, then, that a created being should one day have to give an account of his life to his Creator? People everywhere today are clamouring for justice: justice with wage claims, justice with respect to racial discrimination, justice for the third world. Fair enough! We should be very much concerned about these things. But God also demands justice. If we are concerned about justice, how much more is God! There could be no goodness nor love of God without justice and judgement. And if there were no justice, we should be left with a terrifying meaninglessness of life. Why bother about anything?

The Psalmist in Psalm 73 is taken up with this age-old problem: why do the righteous suffer and the wicked prosper? He starts off with a bare statement of faith, but clearly finds it hard to be convinced about it: 'Truly God is good to the upright, to those who are pure in heart.' He then goes straight on to present his deep-felt problem; 'But as for me, my feet had almost stumbled, my steps had well nigh slipped. For I was envious of the arrogant, when I saw the prosperity of the wicked. For they have no pangs; their bodies are sound and sleek.... Behold these are the wicked; always at ease, they increase in riches.'

The Psalmist then considers his own personal sufferings in spite of his dedication to God: 'All in vain have I kept my heart clean and washed my hands in innocence. For all the day long I have been stricken, and chastened every morning.... But when I thought how to understand this, it seemed to me a wearisome task.' In other words he could not conceive how God could be so monstrously unfair, apparently ignoring his own faith and devotion. At least the perplexity seemed insoluble *'until* I went into the sanctuary of God; then I perceived their end.... How they are destroyed in a moment, swept utterly by terrors! ... My flesh and my heart may fail, but God is the strength of my heart and my portion for ever. For lo, those who are far from thee shall perish; thou dost put an end to those who are false to thee.'

What the Psalmist is saying here is that the mystery of suffering for him was solved when he saw the present 'unfairness' of God in the light of eternity. Once the concept of judgement is included, then indeed there will be vindication of right over wrong, and the problem of injustice becomes less perplexing. Certainly it is because we are living in a world full of suffering and sin and evil and violence and lust and greed that God demands the necessity of justice.

However, as soon as anyone talks about the fact of judgement or the possibility of hell, all sorts of objections are raised.

First, there are *psychological* objections. 'Christ's teaching on judgement and hell produces fear and feelings of guilt. These are unhealthy; and it is bad psychology.' Sometimes in my ministry I hear a distraught mother shouting terrible threats to her unruly children. Is this bad psychology? Yes it is, because these are, I hope, empty threats. There is nothing good to be said about that. But supposing a mother says to a small child, 'Don't run out into the road; you might get run over. Don't go near that fire, you might get burnt.' Is that bad psychology? No! these are healthy and realistic warnings; these tragedies could easily happen. I hope that my son has a healthy fear of fire after he plunged both his hands on to the bars of an electric fire only seconds after it had been turned off. Fear is a very healthy emotion. Phobias are unhealthy, but 'the fear of the Lord is the beginning of wisdom.'

Therefore when Christ warns us repeatedly of the

danger of judgement and hell, is this bad psychology? No! These are wise, healthy and realistic warnings. The tragedies could easily happen.

Secondly, there are *moral* objections. 'Hell is unfair! We have all sinned, and it is unfair that some should spend eternity in heaven whilst others spend eternity in hell, just because of a personal belief in Christ. Surely if anyone is decent, honest, kind and generous, that is all that God could possibly require. In fact, many unbelievers are far nicer than many believers!' I hope that no one would dispute that.

However, the nature of God's judgement is to underline the decision that we make about him. That is not unfair. Indeed it is important to understand exactly what we mean by sin. Sin is described in the Bible by at least five different Greek words, their meaning being:

1 Missing the mark (Greek: hamartia)

It is a word used in archery when the arrow falls short of the target. Sin is therefore the failure to be what we might have been, and could have been. It means falling short of God's purposes and of God's standard for our life. Perhaps the most basic concept of sin is that we live in God's world without reference to God; we use God's gifts without reference to the Giver. We break the first and great commandment. The greatest commandment is to love God with everything we have. The second great commandment is to love other people as ourselves. Now, if we do not love God with all that we have, and if we do not love other people as we should, we have missed the mark. Of course, some people are better than others, humanly speaking. But even though one person might be on the top of Mount Everest in terms of human goodness, while another person is at the bottom of the lowest valley, neither of them can touch the stars. Both have fallen very far short of God's perfect standards shown to us in Jesus Christ. Paul once said, 'For there is no distinction; since all have sinned and fall short of the glory of God.' (Romans 3: 22–23)

2 *Stepping across a line (Greek:* parabasis)

Since God has made us, he has given us the Maker's instructions, seen especially in the Ten Commandments. These are not irrelevant and out of date. They form a clear dividing line between what is right and what is wrong, at least in terms of basic principles; and they are designed for our highest good. If I buy some very complicated piece of machinery, I am free to ignore the maker's instructions if I want to; but I am not free to escape the consequences. Further, God's instructions tell us that our relationship with him should first and foremost be right, and that our relationships with other people should also be right, including our family relationships, our sex relationships, and our behaviour in society.

We are told to treat one another with respect, love, honesty and unselfishness. If then I step across these instructions, I am guilty of sin. Some might protest that they did not know God's standards, but they still have their own standards as is seen by the way in which they criticize and judge other people. Because of this we cannot escape the righteous judgement of God: 'Do you, my friend, pass judgement on others? You have no excuse at all, whoever you are. For when you judge others, but do the same things that they do, you condemn yourself. We know that God is right when he judges the people who do such things as these. But you, my friend, do these very things yourself for which you pass judgement on others! Do you think you will escape God's judgement?' (Romans 2: 1–3 (TEV))

3 *Slipping across a line (Greek:* paraptōma)

This may not be quite so deliberate as the last word, which implies a conscious stepping across a barrier; but because we are naturally sinful we have this bias towards sin. Sometimes in conversation we make a remark that is biting or cutting; it hurts. Later we are often sorry that we have said it, but 'it just slipped out.' That is what we are like.

4 Lawlessness or rebellion (Greek: anōmia)

I go my way not God's way; I do what I want, not what God wants. It is a fundamentally wrong attitude towards God: 'I will not have this man to reign over me!' This, of course, is the really hateful part of sin: when God has given me everything that I possess, life and breath and all things, when God loves me and wants me to know his love and peace and forgiveness, when God has given me his own son Jesus Christ to be my Friend and Saviour, if then I turn my back on God, and say, in effect, 'Stop interfering!', then that is sin.

5 Debt (Greek: opheilēma)

The word refers to sins of omission, which are perhaps the most devastating of all. I once came across a little tract: 'I never was guilty of wrong actions. But on my account lives had been lost, trains had been wrecked, ships had gone down at sea, cities have burned, battles have been lost, and governments have failed. I never struck a blow nor spoke an unkind word, but because of me homes have been broken up, friends have grown cold, the laughter of children has ceased, wives have shed bitter tears, brothers and sisters have forgotten, and fathers and mothers have gone broken-hearted to their graves.' Who am I? I am *neglect*. We do not have to be against God to be in danger of the judgement. We simply have to neglect his offer of life in Jesus Christ. That is the nature of sin. And if, in effect, I say to God now, 'Depart from me,' is it unfair that God should one day reply, 'Depart from me: it is your decision, not mine'? This is the essence of judgement: God gives us what we ourselves have chosen.

Indeed, if it is a case of being unfair at all, we could well say that forgiveness and mercy were unfair. Why should God bother? Why should God forgive? Why should Christ die on the cross in our place? These are the really hard questions to answer. 'To many moderns, that God can punish seems to need explanation. To the early Christians, that God could forgive was the amazing thing.' (Leighton Ford, *The Christian Persuader* (Hodder & Stoughton))

Thirdly, there are *theological* objections. 'I believe in a God of love; I don't believe that he would condemn anyone.' However, as soon as we turn to God's self-revelation in the Scriptures, we may find two surprises. The first surprise is that there is hardly anything about hell in the Old Testament. Some think of the God of the Old Testament as harsh and severe, but in fact there is very little teaching about his final judgement. The second surprise is that there is not much teaching on hell in the epistles of the New Testament. Therefore it is not a corruption of the Gospel by Peter or Paul or John. Indeed, if we want to learn about judgement and hell, we need to turn to the teachings of Jesus himself. And it is a remarkable fact that Jesus, who showed us more than anyone the love of God, also told us more than anyone of the judgement of God. The theologian Jeremias once wrote, 'The message of Jesus is not only the proclamation of salvation, but also the announcement of judgement, a cry of warning, and a call to repentance in view of the terrible urgency of the crises. The number of parables in this category is nothing less than awe-inspiring.'

Why did Jesus of all people speak in such solemn terms? Partly, I believe, because the teaching is so severe that we might not take it except from someone who so manifestly loved and cared. Partly also, because in his love and care Jesus spoke frankly about our greatest need, and did something about it at the cost of his own life. If I find someone lying in the road with a broken leg, what love do I show him if I simply say, 'I see your shoelace is undone; let me tie it for you' – and then walk off! True love will always care about the deepest and most urgent needs, and do something about them.

Indeed, I do not believe that we shall ever understand the wonder of God's love except in the context of judgement. Perhaps the greatest love verse in the Bible is John 3:16, 'For God so loved the world that he gave his only Son, that whoever believes in him *should not perish* but have eternal life.' The astonishing measure of God's love is that we all deserve to perish, because we have broken his laws so often. But he so loved the world, including you and me, that we need not perish but find in his Son eternal life. God knows that naturally we are all going down a broad road which leads to destruction. In his love he sets before us one obstacle after another to stop us going along that road. He gives us the Bible, Christian books, Christian friends, Christian churches, and above all the outstretched arms of Jesus on the cross. If I choose to run past all those obstacles, then I have only myself to blame for the consequences. It is part of the essence and tragedy of love that it risks being rejected. It is simply shallow thinking to say that the judgement of God is inconsistent with the love of God. It is because God loves that he will not force, and therefore there is the terrifying possibility of rejecting and forfeiting his love. If I choose to do that, I have automatically chosen his judgement instead. If I do not want God, I do not have God. If I want to be on my own, I shall be on my own. This is the first principle of hell. It is perfectly fair, and quite consistent with a God of love.

Having looked at some of the objections, let us consider two questions.

1 What will be the criterion of judgement?

Christ made it clear that judgement would always be according to opportunity. Those who have never heard about Christ can still know something about God through creation, and conscience. They will therefore be judged by the moral judgements that they have made about other people, for by these judgements they clearly have some sense of right and wrong. Again it is perfectly fair. But who has lived up even to his own standards in life, let alone God's? However, as the Swiss theologian René Pache has expressed it, 'God does not allow any of his creatures to be eternally lost, without, in his own way, seeking to win them. Thus when the time comes to leave the world, every man has had enough light to have accepted or rejected God, so that he is fully responsible to him.'

For those who have heard about Christ, the position is quite clear. We shall be judged according to our response to Christ and our relationship with him. What have we done with God's Son? What place have we given to God's greatest gift to us? That will be the criterion of judgement; and to many he will have to say 'I never knew you, depart from me.' (Matthew 7: 23)

2 What will be the nature of judgement?

The answer, for those who have not responded to Christ, is eternal separation from God and from everything good. And to stress the seriousness of this Christ used one solemn expression after another. Further, when we see him weeping over the city of Jerusalem because of its coming judgement, and when we see Christ's own appalling agony on the cross, it is quite certain that he was not playing with words when he spoke about the dangers of 'outer darkness.'

Further, if anyone is still baffled to see how suffering and hell are consistent with a God of love, we need to look carefully at God's own revelation in terms of his Son Jesus Christ. Christ not only taught repeatedly that God is a God of love, but he had a perfect relationship of love with his own Father. He spoke often of the Father loving the Son and the Son loving the Father. More than that, he showed the love of God by his immense compassion. He cared for individuals in all their ugliness and needs. He had compassion on lepers and outcasts, prostitutes and thieves, the deaf and dumb and blind and lame. He loved Zacchaeus, the cheat whom everybody despised. He cared for the Samaritan woman whom so many had used. He washed the feet of his own disciples. He prayed even for his murderers; and whilst hanging on the cross, in excruciating pain, he cared for the personal needs of his own mother, and brought peace and forgiveness to one of the thieves crucified with him. Everywhere we see the love of Jesus, or the love of God as expressed in his own Son.

At the same time, everywhere we see suffering too. He was born in poverty, despised and rejected by men, a man of sorrows and acquainted with grief. He was misunderstood, slandered and hated. He knew oppression, loneliness, torture, and the most agonising death reserved for the very worst of criminals. 'Surely he has borne our griefs and carried our sorrows; yet we esteemed him stricken, smitten by God, and afflicted. ... He was oppressed, and he was afflicted, yet he opened not his mouth; like a lamb that is led to the slaughter, and like a sheep that before its shearers is dumb, so he opened not his mouth.' (Isaiah 53: 4, 7)

William Temple once explained the problem like this, ' "There cannot be a God of love," men say, "because if there was, and he looked upon the world, his heart would break." The church points to the cross and says, "It did break." "It is God who made the world," men say. "It is he who should bear the load." The church points to the cross and says, "He did bear it." '

Indeed, when it comes to the question of judgement and hell, nowhere can the reality of these be seen more clearly than on the cross: 'He was wounded for our transgressions, he was bruised for our iniquities; upon him was the chastisement that made us whole, and with his stripes we are healed. All we like sheep have gone astray; we have turned everyone to his own way; and the Lord has laid on him the iniquity of us all.' (Isaiah 53: 5–6) Listen to Jesus's cry of intense suffering, 'My God, my God, why have you forsaken me?' The precise significance of these words can be lost by their familiarity. The essence of sin is to forsake God; therefore the consequence of sin is to be God-forsaken. God underlies our decision and gives us what we want. That is the nature of hell: to be God-forsaken. And such is the love of God that his own Son suffered hell on the cross for us, that we might be forgiven and loved and

brought to know the love of God in our own sinful, rebellious hearts. That is the supreme demonstration that,
even in the midst of suffering and hell, God is a God of
love. 'In the long run,' writes C S Lewis, 'the answer to
all those who object to the doctrine of hell is itself a
question: "What are you asking God to do?" To wipe
out their past sins and, at all costs, to give them a fresh
start, smoothing every difficulty and offering every
miraculous help? But he has done so, on Calvary.' (*The
Problem of Pain* (Fontana))

5
The Revolution of Love

If there is nothing more basic than love, there is nothing more obvious than the revolution of love which has changed so much of society in recent years. At least, that is true of the sex revolution, which dominates the scene today. The question is whether this revolution of sex can rightly be called a revolution of love; and how does it compare with the Christian concept of love, as seen in Jesus Christ.

Much personal counselling today is concerned with the relationships that have gone wrong. Indeed, the major tragedy in terms of relationships is that we so often use one another. We may call it 'love'; but it is a travesty of the real meaning of love if I 'love' a person for what I can get out of that person. Of course, we would hotly deny that we are doing this. 'I really love her,' we say; 'I would do anything for her!' No doubt that is true, providing that all is going well. But the fact remains that society today is littered with broken relationships, broken promises, broken hearts, broken homes, broken marriages, broken lives and often broken health. Why? Because all too often we *use* people to satisfy our needs. Especially this is true with the revolution of sex.

'Because of the pill,' said Dr Helena Wright, 'we are at last able to free human sexual capacities. If a person is capable of responding to three or four partners, that's a rich personality!' (*Sunday Telegraph*, 30 November

1969) This means that I could become a rich personality by *using* three or four different partners. Why not? Perhaps they are *using* me. It is all part of the sex revolution of today.

Of course, there is nothing new in all this. You will find a rampantly permissive society as far back as Genesis 6. And in New Testament times there was an almost total disregard of sexual morality. A Roman Empress in AD 50 was a common prostitute; of the first fifteen Roman Emperors, fourteen were practising homosexuals; and Jerome tells of a woman marrying her twenty-third husband, she being his twenty-first wife!

However, within the last century the pendulum in the West has swung from one extreme to the other. Whereas the charge levelled at the Victorians was 'love without sex,' today it is 'sex without love.' A modern poet describes the physical and emotional experience, totally devoid of any real relationship:

> *The Act of Love lies somewhere*
> *Between the belly and the mind*
> *I lost the love some time ago*
> *Now I've only the act to grind*
>
> *Brought her back from a party*
> *Don't bother swopping names*
> *Identity's not needed*
> *When you are only playing games*
>
> *High on bedroom darkness*
> *We endure the pantomime*
> *Ships that go bump in the night*
> *Run aground on the sands of time*
>
> *Saved in the nick of dawn*
> *It's cornflakes and then goodbye*
> *Another notch on the headboard*
> *Another day wondering why*
>
> *The Act of Love lies somewhere*
> *Between the belly and the mind*
> *I lost the love some time ago*
> *Now I have only the act to grind.*

© Roger McGough 1967

What's wrong? Why accept a bourgeois morality? Why conform to middle class values? Many young people today are rightly exposing this morality as having no basis for its values, that is no basis apart from convention. So many are seeing very clearly (and this is perfectly fair), that these standards by themselves, without any solid basis, are arbitrary, traditional, or bourgeois. Therefore one obvious reaction is to destroy the system. Who cares? Why shouldn't I? What's to stop me? These are perfectly valid questions.

In fact, the only solid answer to these questions is that God has given us standards of behaviour which are not arbitrary. They are good and right, and expressions of his love. Because he is a God of love, he has shown us the greatest meaning of love, and the best possible relationship that we can have with one another. Thus we need to look carefully at God's standards in terms of personal relationships, as revealed in the Bible and as taught supremely by Jesus Christ. And if you think that the Bible is anti-sex you are very much mistaken. It sees sex as one of the greatest gifts given to us by our Creator, an expression of his creative work of love, and the most intimate token of love between a man and a woman that they can possibly have. There are many magnificent statements about sex relationships in the Bible, not least in the Song of Solomon, one of the most beautiful love poems that you can find anywhere in ancient literature.

God's standards are definite

In the first place, God's standards are quite definite. There is nothing ambiguous about them, which is why Christ's teaching is so unacceptable and unpopular in certain quarters. Basically there is one clear principle: *sex outside marriage is out*. The biblical standard is chastity before marriage and fidelity after marriage. 'Let marriage be held in honour among all, and let the marriage bed be undefiled; for God will judge the immoral and adulterous.' (Hebrews 13:4) Further, Jesus not only endorsed those standards, which go back to Old Testament days; he applied them to our thoughts and imaginations as well as to our actions. 'You have heard that it was said, "You shall not commit adultery." But I say to you that everyone who looks at a woman lustfully has already committed adultery with her in his heart.' (Matthew 5:27f) This of course hammers the hypocrisy which makes the open and outward behaviour so important, regardless of private thoughts and deeds.

God's standards are right and good

In the second place, God's standards are right and good. God is no spoil-sport! It is not just a matter of 'Thou shalt not! Thou shalt not! Thou shalt not!' Far from it. God is the Maker of sex, and therefore in its rightful place sex is very beautiful indeed. Jesus once said that eternal life means knowing God, and the word for 'knowing' is a word that is quite often used in the Bible in terms of a sexual relationship. This intimate human bond is frequently a picture in the Bible of the deep spiritual bond which an individual can have with his Creator.

Indeed it is precisely because sex is so beautiful that God, the Maker of sex, has given us the Maker's instructions. And centuries of history have proved that his instructions are absolutely right. The Harvard sociologist, Professor P A Sorokin, in his book *The American Sex Revolution*, describes the Russian attitude of the '20s: 'The revolution leaders deliberately attempted to destroy marriage and the family. The legal distinction between marriage and casual sexual intercourse was abolished. Bigamy and polygamy were permissible under the new provisions. Abortion was facilitated in the state institutions. Pre-marital relationships were praised; extra-marital relationships were considered normal.... Within a few years millions of lives, especially of young girls, were wrecked. The hatred and conflicts ... rapidly mounted and so did psychoneuroses. Work in the nationalized factories slackened. The government was forced to reverse its policy.' Indeed, Russia has returned to very strict standards of sexual morality.

China, too, is outwardly a clean and moral country, sexually speaking. Further, these atheistic states have not only returned to the Maker's instructions, which they have had to learn the hard way, but they now enforce them in the strongest possible terms. They see a sex revolution as one of the greatest threats for any society. Today's revolutionaries know this, of course. The Yippie leader, Jerry Rubin, once said, 'We aim to splinter society by a combination of sex and violence and drugs.' Indeed in Russia and China pornography is regarded as a sign of the 'decadence of the capitalist system.'

Moreover, on a personal basis, God really does know what he is talking about in his instructions. One girl told me that she had felt for years 'as guilty as hell' because of her free and easy sex experiences. Several couples have come to me with serious problems in their sex relationships within marriage, simply because of their free love experiences outside marriage. Free sex does not increase a person's capacity for love and sex; very much the reverse.

Abortion too presents desperate problems. On my way to a meeting I was handed a Women's Lib tract called *Enlightenment*. It said 'Woman's Liberation demands control over her own body and her own destiny, free contraceptives and free abortion on demand....' Is this really enlightenment? What is the value of human life and where is the meaning of love if there is free abortion on demand? What is the meaning of life when the first stages of life can be destroyed so readily in the interests of sex? We have not even considered all the other attendant problems. According to one report, venereal disease is now the commonest disease apart from the common cold.

When God says, 'Save sex for marriage,' he is not trying to frustrate us. He wants us to know the greatest possible joy. A parachutist should not complain of instructions not to jump unless he has put on his parachute. The advice is simply for his own good. He may, of course, decide to jump with no strings attached. He is free to ignore the instructions. He is free to jump if he wants to. But he is not free to escape the consequences.

I know of one girl, and probably there are thousands like her, who told me that she continues to sleep with her boyfriend because she is afraid that otherwise she would lose him. Here is a relationship, supposedly of love, which already is being spoilt by fear and mistrust and uncertainty. There is no firm commitment. And if the moral fence has once been jumped, how can you be sure that it will not happen again? So often it does. Victor Brown in *A Kind of Loving* said, 'To get really free, though, I have to get right away from her, because while I am still with her I have got that feeling that I am just about the rottenest devil alive for treating her this way.' So many experience such tensions.

God's standards are not easy

In the third place God's standards are not easy for us. None of the best things in life are easy. Therefore 'free love,' when referring to sexual relationships, is a contradiction in terms: if it is free, it is not love; if it is love, it is not free. A woman doctor put it like this: 'Our thirteen-year old can now pass happily from boy to boy with no fear, except the knowledge that it is not love that she is giving or receiving, frustrated that the act of procreation is of her choice, degraded as she knows she is only an article to be used and discarded. The whole gamut of emotions released must be thwarted and stilted – the only reward is orgasm.' (*Pornography, The Longford Report*)

Temporary sexual relationships so often mean acting a lie. A person wants the expression of love, in terms of sex, without the reality of love in terms of responsibilities. If I really love a girl, I must express that love for her by giving my whole life to her, not by giving her or getting from her a few moments of sexual pleasure; nor by agreeing, even mutually, to opt out of the relationship if things are difficult. Real love involves firm commitment. Real love, with any depth, will grow and develop through difficulties in that commitment. The self-control and discipline and forgiveness that are so often needed within a true and lasting relationship are the very factors which develop a really mature and beautiful love relationship. Sex is only a temporary physical expression of the much greater bond of love itself.

I have often been asked 'What's wrong with a steady partner, especially if we are probably going to get married one day anyway?' Here it is not a question of promiscuity, with all its serious risks of VD; it is simply pre-marital intercourse, because, for one reason or another, a marriage is not yet possible or convenient. Therefore why not sleep together, with a steady or serious partner? My answer very briefly is this.

First, you cannot escape the possibility of pregnancy; and the British Medical Association says that the fear of pregnancy, which is very widespread, is a threat to mental health and academic work. Further, both abortion and unwanted babies present immense problems. There is only one completely safe form of contraception, and it is the cheapest. It is to say no!

Second, where there is no binding commitment, as in a marriage service, there will nearly always be an element of fear in the relationship – the fear of losing him or her. And fear is the opposite of love.

Third, in sex before marriage there is nearly always a degree of selfishness and greed: 'I must have this *now*!' This leads to a lack of self-respect, and I do not know of anyone who later has felt that they have gained by it.

Fourth, although we dress it up in high sounding phrases such as 'pre-marital intercourse,' Jesus called it fornication and sin. It breaks God's laws, and no one can do that without paying the consequences sooner or later.

This is love

If we want to understand the real meaning of love, we must look carefully at both the teaching and the life of Jesus Christ. Jesus mixed with the most progressive and permissive society of his day. He was loved by prostitutes and drunkards, yet he himself was absolutely pure. He was 'tempted in every way that we are, but did not sin.' (Hebrews 4: 15 (TEV)) That is why he was and is so attractive. Let us therefore look more closely at God's love as shown to us in Christ.

In the first place,

Love is concerned with people

Jesus was not in the least concerned about himself and his own selfish desires. He put all that totally on one side. Never once do we find a trace of him using people for his own selfish ends. Always he went out in love and compassion to people as people, individual people, each one vitally important to God. Many of them were not very lovable: traitors and cheats, prostitutes and pimps, the social outcasts of his day, the drop-outs and rejects of society, the unwanted and the unloved. Sometimes, too, he came to the rich and influential, the religious and respectful. And he came to everybody with love, friendship, understanding and forgiveness. Indeed, his enemies, intending it as an abuse, called him, 'the friend of sinners.' But that was and is the most wonderful fact about him. 'This is what love is: it is not that we have loved God, but that he loved us and sent his Son to be the means by which our sins are forgiven.' (1 John 4: 1 (TEV)) Therefore he reaches out to us, whoever we may be or whatever we may have done. If you have made rather a mess of your sex life, Jesus loves you. If you have not made a mess of your sex life, Jesus loves you. If you feel totally unworthy of him, Jesus loves you. If you feel no need of him at all, Jesus loves you. Whatever our actions or attitudes might be, God takes the initiative and reaches out to us in love through his Son Jesus Christ.

That is the most wonderful truth. A friend of mine is a professional actress, attractive, loving, and a beautiful personality. She must have had many friends all her life. A little time ago she found Jesus as her personal Friend and she said that she has never experienced such love before in her life.

This personal love of Jesus for individuals is, of course, very striking. You may follow the teachings of Karl Marx, Buddha, Bertrand Russell, the Divine Light, or anyone else that you might mention. But not one of those individuals will love you personally. Many of them are dead anyway. But you can know the love of Jesus in your own personal experience.

In the second place,

Love satisfies the deepest needs of people
It is not content with superficial problems; it is concerned to tackle the real problems and to satisfy the depths of our being. One of the tragedies of human relationships, especially as seen in terms of sex, is that these cannot possibly satisfy in any complete or lasting way. The really deep needs for forgiveness, purpose, peace, go completely unfulfilled. With human love, we are always wanting more and more and more. Jesus once said to a woman well-known in Samaria for her popularity with men, 'You'll thirst again!' In other words you will never satisfy your deepest thirst from your outside world, because your inside world is empty and dry, crying out for peace and for love. Sex will never give a person that. If anything it will make our deepest thirst more acute than ever before: 'You will thirst again!' 'But,' said Jesus, 'whoever drinks the water that I shall give him will never thirst; the water that I shall give him will become in him a spring of water welling up to eternal life.' (John 4: 14)

In the third place,

Love is willing for sacrifice

Jesus made that quite clear, both by his teaching and by his example. He told us to forgive and forgive and forgive – seventy times seven. He told us to love our enemies and to pray for those who made life difficult for us, to give without any hope of return, and to get involved with the needs of people. It is one thing to get involved in causes (an easy alternative); but it is quite another thing to get involved with people, needy and demanding people. Someone has described the sort of love which is all too common today like this: 'I was hungry and you formed a committee to investigate my hunger. I was homeless and you filed a report of my plight. I was sick and you held a seminar on the situation of the underprivileged. You have investigated all aspects of my plight; and yet I am still hungry, homeless and sick.'

Not so Jesus! So great was his love for people that he himself was often hungry and homeless, tired and lonely. He prayed for his enemies, and he gave himself all the time to bring his love to men and women and children with all their complicated needs. He even gave his life, on the cross, to take away our sins. And there on the cross all our sin, guilt and filth was taken by Jesus so that every single one of us might know God's forgiveness and peace. That is the measure of his love.

It is so easy talking about the cross. But try to imagine Jesus – the loveliest man that ever lived, gentle and compassionate, honest and true – being crucified for your sins.

Certainly there was *physical* pain. Jesus was whipped with leather thongs to which sharp pieces of metal or bone had been fastened, ripping his flesh. Many victims died from this scourging alone. He staggered on the road, carrying the instrument of his execution; and when he was held down on the cross, huge nails and spikes were driven through the palms of his hands and his feet. The cross was then lifted up and dropped into the hole prepared for it. There Jesus hung, with the heat, thirst, flies and gnats, and the searing, stabbing pain shooting through every nerve of his body. It was excruciatingly painful.

On top of that Jesus experienced *mental* agony. After all, he had come to love people with a degree and intensity of love that we have scarcely ever known. What happened? They mocked him, despised him, rejected him and crucified him. Think for a moment of the person you love most of all in this world. Imagine your feelings if that person mocked you, despised, rejected and crucified you! If you can imagine such an appalling thing, you will have a glimpse of the mental sufferings of Jesus when he died for your sins.

Worst of all was the *spiritual* torment, as he took the full weight and penalty of our sins upon himself that we might be free to know God's love. We could never fully understand the horror of that spiritual alienation from God that Jesus experienced when he cried out 'My God, my God, why have you forsaken me?' But, in a word, it was hell – total spiritual anguish, in order that *we* might forever enjoy the peace and freedom of God's gracious presence. Peter once said, 'Christ also died for sins once for all, the righteous for the unrighteous, that he might bring us to God.' (1 Peter 3:18) Paul wrote, 'God shows his love for us in that while we were yet sinners Christ died for us.' (Romans 5:8)

In the fourth place,

Love requires a response

Love always does! When I proposed to that lovely person who has now become my wife, I said 'Will you?' I was expecting an answer, yes or no. It might have been 'wait,' but that is a risky response. There may not be another opportunity! When, therefore, Jesus says 'Will you?' offering you both himself and his love, it is a terribly important moment. We are told in the Bible to 'seek the Lord while he may be found, call upon him while he is near.' (Isaiah 55 : 6) There are certain moments in a person's life when God is especially to be found, and he is very near. He waits for our response. He will not force us, because he loves us. We are quite free to ignore him or to reject him. But we are not free to escape the consequences. Therefore in his love he is urgent.

Having known the reality of the love of Jesus in my own life for many years, and having seen this revolution of love taking place in the lives of hundreds and thousands of people whom I have personally met or known, I can never, never understand why some people do not want to get involved. There is nothing so beautiful or totally satisfying as the love of Jesus. It is always fresh and new, and it is a love which never fails.

6
Death and the Occult

What happens at death? It is the one question we cannot escape, because death is the one event that we must all face. George Bernard Shaw once wrote in characteristic fashion, 'Death is the ultimate statistic: one out of one dies.' What then happens at death? Job asked 3,000 years ago, 'If a man dies, shall he live again?' Tennyson longed for 'the touch of a vanished hand and the sound of a voice that is still.'

Today, in spite of all our progress, most people are thoroughly confused concerning the question of death. Usually there is an astonishing silence about this subject. Fifty years ago everyone talked realistically about death, but no one talked about sex. Today everyone talks about sex, but very few talk about death, unless they have to; and then so often they do so in veiled clichés. Indeed, we fight death for all we are worth, with pills and prescriptions, transplants and treatments; and just in case the 'worst' should happen, there are of course insurance policies and pension schemes. 'If you had died yesterday, what would you be worth today?' This was an advertisement in the national press, and a thought-provoking question. It was, in fact, put out by an insurance company, urging you to make your death worthwhile for at least someone!

Some years ago David Frost devoted one of his programmes to the theme of death. A panel of celebrities had been arranged, and each was asked to state his views. In many ways it was a most unsatisfactory programme, but at least two things emerged. In the first place there was almost total confusion and haziness about death. 'I think that possibly, perhaps, or maybe ...' No one had any clear ideas. In the second place almost everyone was frightened of death for one reason or another. Indeed, someone has said that 'the fear of death is so natural that all life is one long effort not to think about it.'

That is no doubt why it is one of the non-topics of conversation today. Apart from the Christian faith, there are no real answers at all in the face of death. Therefore the vast majority of people are afraid to die: not perhaps when they are discussing it in a detached way, sitting comfortably in an armchair and talking pleasantly with their friends; but when face to face with man's final enemy most people deep down are afraid.

A young person once expressed it like this:

> I lie awake worrying what it will be like to be
>   dead
> I lie awake worrying how dark the coffin will be.
> I lie awake and feel how cold my life will be.
> It makes no sense the end of life being death.
> Just a memory, and then nothing,
> Absolutely nothing, just nothing.
> Death is like a black hole without any sides.
> Death is like a thought without a thinker.
> Death is fear....

What causes this fear at death? It is primarily the fear of the unknown. At death we are cut off from the world that we know and the people that we love. 'We brought nothing into this world, and it is certain that we carry nothing out.' We leave behind our home, our family, our friends, our possessions – everything.

What happens at death? The answer to that question affects not only our death but the whole of our life. Carl Jung once wrote, 'The question of the meaning and the worth of life never becomes more urgent or more agonising than when we see the final breath leave a body which a moment before was living.' An extraordinary comment! The urgent questions about life come at death! Here is a body that has just died. What is different? It all looks remarkably the same. Philosophers have always maintained that the key to life is to be found in coming to terms with death. No man can live until he can die well, for he might be living in a fool's paradise. I once talked with a medical student who had just dissected his first human body. The corpse had been there in front of him, and he had cut away different parts of the anatomy. It was like a wax model. 'If this is all that we become at death, what is the point of anything?' he asked. Has life any ultimate purpose? Or is it in the last analysis, earth to earth, ashes to ashes, dust to dust? What happens at death?

There are, of course, many theories, and we need to look at a few of them briefly.

Certainly *atheism* has no answer. The atheist says categorically, 'nothing happens after death.' In some famous words of Bertrand Russell, in his book *Why I am not a Christian*, 'When I die I shall rot, and nothing of my ego will survive.... There is darkness without and when I die there will be darkness within. There is no splendour, no vastness anywhere: only triviality for a moment, and then nothing.' In many ways this is an appalling philosophy. If when a person dies, he must say to those whom he loves 'I shall never see you again'; if he just rots in the grave; if there is no heaven, no vindication of right over wrong, no hope whatever concerning the future, this is not only a philosophy of total despair, but it makes nonsense of any true purpose in life.

If that were true, why bother about anything at all? 'One day I, too, will be dead and snow will fall on my tomb, while the living will laugh, embrace and enjoy life. I shall be unable to participate in their joys; I shall not even know them. I will simply not exist any more. After a short time no one will remember me. So what use is anything?' (*In God's Underground* by Richard

Wurmbrand (W H Allen))

It is important to realize, however, that the atheist's view is pure theory. He has no clear evidence to support it. Indeed, as we shall see in a moment, all the solid, substantial, historical evidence is against him, in particular the person and teaching and resurrection of Jesus Christ.

Secondly, *mysticism* has no answers. In an interview with the Maharishi Mahesh Yogi, of Beatle fame, the interviewer, Dennis Hart, tried to find out about the Maharishi's Master, Guru Dev. 'Where is he now?' he asked a teacher. 'Well, he died.' 'Yes, I know, but where is he now?' He was told, 'That is a philosophical and theosophical question I am not qualified to answer.'

Not satisfied he tried again, asking the Maharishi's closest lieutenant, Max Fisher, once a lecturer in London: 'Where is Guru Dev now?' 'Maharishi never speaks about that. Maharishi has got rid of all belief. By now I have had enough glimpses of myself (which is universal) to be able to ignore the question of the cessation of a limited self-hood. Those glimpses are so powerful that they may take over the whole of your life, and you feel identified with that universal self-hood.'

Understandably not satisfied, the interviewer asked the Maharishi himself: 'Where is Guru Dev, now that he is dead?' Sublimely the answer came, 'When the boundaries relax, what remains is the boundless.'

What does all that mean? What is the evidence for it? What hope does it give a man who is dying? What comfort can it bring to those who are bereaved? It is fairly obvious that the mystic has no real answer when confronted with death.

Thirdly, *universalism* gives no true answer, though it attractively suggests that everyone is welcomed into heaven, regardless of his response to God the Father or God the Son during his life-time. It might be comforting to believe this, but there are various problems with this theory. In the first place it makes nonsense of heaven, if heaven were full of those who wanted to have nothing to do with God when they were here on earth: Hitlers, Satanists and all the God-haters down the ages. In the second place it makes nonsense of man's freedom: if we are free now to reject God's love, but one day forced to accept it, then what is the meaning of our freedom? In the third place it makes nonsense of the person and teaching of Jesus Christ. Jesus taught so clearly that there would one day be a judgement to come, when we should be either eternally with God or eternally separated from God. If that were not true, then the warnings of Jesus would become dishonest attempts to frighten us into faith. 'He becomes like the very worst sort of school teacher who, having failed to make his subject intrinsically attractive, and being without any personal charm to make up for this deficiency, resorts to threats, which at last he lacks the strength of character to enforce.' (*After Death* by Alec Motyer (Hodder & Stoughton)) Everything about Christ, his love and humility and honesty and integrity, utterly discounts that theory.

Fourth, *reincarnation* is no answer. For some it may seem to be an attractive theory, although I am not sure that everyone wants to reappear on this earth, and finally lose his identity by being absorbed into some universal consciousness! But the main argument against reincarnation is that it is contrary to the teaching of Christ. Repeatedly he made it clear that at death there would be a great separation between those who know Christ and those who do not. After that it will be impossible to change sides. In Luke 16: 19ff Jesus spoke about two men who died, one who went to heaven and the other who went to hell. The one in hell now realized his tragic mistake throughout his life, and cried out for mercy. But he was told that between heaven and hell there was 'a great chasm fixed in order that those who would pass from here to you may not be able, and none may cross from there to us.' The Bible is totally silent about any possibility of reincarnation, and there is no evidence for any second chance after death. Indeed the positive teaching is that 'it is appointed for men to die once and after that comes judgement.' (Hebrews 9: 27)

Fifthly, *spiritualism* has no answers in the face of death. It is understandable why some turn to spiritualism, especially after the death of a friend or relative whom they have loved, and sometimes comforting messages are received. What can we say about this?

The occult

We need to look for a moment at the whole question of the occult. The word means secret or dark or mysterious, something which transcends our ordinary world of five senses. Although there is a huge variety of occult practices, they can be divided into three main sections. First there is *fortune telling*, such as astrology, palmistry, clairvoyance, divination, rod and pendulum, colour therapy, and radiesthesia. All forms of fortune telling are increasingly popular today, with books on astrology booming and horoscopes to be found everywhere. In the USA there are 1,750 daily newspapers; and in 1,220 you will find each day a horoscope. In Paris, according to *Time* magazine, there is one priest for every 5,000, one doctor for every 514, and one spiritualist for every 120.

In the second place there is *magic* which involves the manipulation of supernatural powers for various purposes such as charms and curses. Although there is a distinction between black and white magic, both come under the overall heading of the occult.

In the third place there is *spiritism* or spirit-communication, such as table lifting, glass moving, ouija boards, and automatic writing.

It is worth noting that the principles and practices of occultism are the same today as they were 5,000 years ago. Yet in this sophisticated space-age, it is becoming more and more popular. In recent years Britain has become the world centre of occultism, and Americans have organised 'psychic' package tours to London.

Witchcraft has also developed considerably, and according to various reports there are several thousand practising witches in Great Britain alone.

Why do we find this astonishing resurgence of occult practice in an age of science and technology? Partly it is because no one, apart from Jesus Christ and the Christian faith, has any solid answers at all in the face of death. Further, most people are hungry for God or for some sort of spiritual reality, because God has made them that way. Materialism does not satisfy, and cannot answer the vital questions of life. However, sometimes the Church, in its formal traditional establishment, has appeared irrelevant and remote. Two students once explained to me why they had turned to spiritualism. They complained that they had been to many religious meetings in churches, but always it had been words, words, words, They were now sick of words, and they were seriously searching for spiritual realities. They claimed that they had found this at a seance.

What can we say of the dangers of occultism? Some phenomena, of course, may be quite spurious and easily explained away, but no doubt much of it is both real and dangerous. One of the leading spiritists in America said that he did not know a single case of spiritism where there had not been distinct deterioration of physical, mental or spiritual faculties.

One minister tried to discredit occult practices as mere superstition, and paid a large sum for a sophisticated horoscope in order to prove that it did not work. For eight years he became increasingly disturbed as the predictions were fulfilled to the smallest detail. He found it hard to pray, and worship and Bible reading became increasingly difficult. He came to the conclusion that he had placed himself under some occult and evil power. Finally he renounced the horoscope and asked God's forgiveness for having dabbled with the occult. From that moment onwards, the horoscope became inaccurate for him. His personal experience of God was restored.

A friend of mine was called in to help five students who had only recently started playing with a ouija board. Although to begin with it was no more than a party game, they soon experienced a series of strange and frightening events. One of the girls became violent and even tried to kill another member of the group. Soon they were seriously affected both mentally and physically, and for three weeks were unable to attend their college lectures. Later they were all set free by the power of Jesus Christ, but it had been a most distressing experience.

The evidence is that any person who dabbles in the occult is playing with something dangerous and destructive, which can lead to tragic situations, and from which there is no final deliverance, except through the power of Christ. We should not be surprised by this, because there are almost fifty references to the occult in the Bible and every time it is described as being thoroughly evil and offensive to God. 'There shall not be found among you anyone who burns his son or his daughter as an offering, anyone who practises divination, a soothsayer, or an augur, or a sorcerer, or a charmer, or a medium, or a wizard, or a necromancer (= spiritualist). For whoever does these things is an abomination to the Lord; and because of these abominable practices the Lord your God is driving them out before you.... For these nations, which you are about to dispossess, give heed to soothsayers and to diviners; but as for you, the Lord your God has not allowed you so to do.' (Deuteronomy 18: 10–14)

In his book *Occult Bondage and Deliverance* (Evangelization Publishers, Germany), Dr Kurt E Koch says, 'For years I have witnessed the truth of this fact, that magic and almost all other occult practices either destroy the Christian faith of a person or just prevent it from developing. And yet one finds that there is no conflict between sorcery and all the other world religions.' This is a particularly interesting point. It is only when these evil powers come face to face with God's truth in the person of Jesus Christ that there is a serious conflict.

In God's eyes, therefore, all forms of spiritualism and occultism are out. 'When they say to you "Consult the mediums and the wizards who chirp and mutter," should not a people consult their God? Should they consult the dead on behalf of the living? To the teaching and the testimony! (i.e. the Scriptures). Surely for this word which they (the mediums) speak there is no dawn.' (Isaiah 8: 19-20) Certainly there is 'no dawn' from spiritism: no light at all about life after death. However, in this context, with the darkness that we still have in the face of death, and with meaninglessness and hopelessness of so much of life, we have this glorious prophecy in the very next few verses: 'The people who walked in darkness have seen a great light; those who dwelt in a land of deep darkness, on them has light shined.... For to us a child is born, to us a son is given; and the government will be upon his shoulder, and his name will be called "Wonderful Counsellor, Mighty God, Everlasting Father, Prince of Peace."' (Isaiah 9: 2, 6)

Why go after dark and dangerous spirits when you can find in Jesus a Wonderful Counsellor? Why pursue unknown forces when you can find in Jesus the Mighty God, and know him as your everlasting Father? Why get involved with things that may very much disturb you when in Jesus you can know the Prince of Peace?

Moreover, these questions are not just for those involved in spiritism. The Bible makes it clear that the whole world naturally is in the hands of the evil one, the devil. Jesus once said to some very religious and respectable people, 'You are of your father the devil!' (John 8: 44) They were shocked! However, he said that, not because they were very evil (by most external standards they were extremely good); but because they could not yet call God their Father. You can call God your 'Father,' only when you have received Jesus into your life. 'To all who received him, who believed in his name, he gave power to become children of God.' (John 1 : 12) This is why Jesus kept on calling people out of Satan's kingdom into God's kingdom, out of Satan's family into God's family. Only in God's family can you find light and love and forgiveness and peace in any real and lasting sense.

What, then, happens at death? Is there any answer when there are no satisfactory answers at all from atheism, mysticism, universalism, reincarnation or spiritualism? You can understand why those first Christians leapt to their feet and shouted from the housetops the most wonderful and glorious news that Jesus had been raised from the dead. Not only was he alive and with them all; but now they realized that through his death and resurrection he had destroyed death! They were absolutely convinced about it. They were willing to suffer and die for what they knew was true. Why were they so sure? Why are millions of Christians so sure today? What is the evidence that has made countless millions of people over 2,000 years convinced that Jesus rose from the dead and is alive for ever?

Other books have set forth the evidence in much greater detail, such as *The Evidence for the Resurrection, Christianity the Witness of History* by J N D Anderson (IVP), *Man Alive* by Michael Green (IVP), *Who Moved the Stone?* by Frank Morrison (Faber). Briefly it is worth considering the following points:

First, we have the birth and growth of the Christian Church. The disciples of Jesus were utterly despondent after the crucifixion of Christ. They had no understanding at all, in spite of repeated teaching, that Jesus would be raised from the dead. There was not a glimmer of hope. To them, after that appalling Friday, he was finished and gone. They would never see him again. Indeed, when the first reports came on the Sunday that the tomb was empty and that Jesus had been seen alive, the apostles dismissed this as old wives' tales. It was idle talk. Nothing would shake their gloom and sorrow. Now, in that context, it is historically and psychologically impossible that those disciples could suddenly have been filled with such conviction and joy that Jesus had indeed been raised from the dead, that they turned their world upside down, as their enemies had to confess. At least this is impossible if Jesus had not been raised.

Secondly, the New Testament could never have been written without the resurrection of Christ. Throughout its pages there is the total assurance that Jesus was and is alive, and the books of the New Testament were written at least 20 years after the death of Christ, following periods of considerable persecution, when this conviction had plenty of time to waver and die. As J B Phillips records in *Ring of Truth* (Hodder & Stoughton), after years spent on translating these documents: 'These (New Testament) letters were written over quite a period of years, but there is not the slightest discernible diminution of faith. It was borne in upon me with irresistible force that these letters could never have been written at all if there had been no Jesus Christ, no crucifixion, and no resurrection.'

Thirdly, there is the evidence of the empty tomb. The message of the risen Christ could not have been maintained in Jerusalem for a single day if the emptiness of the tomb and the disappearance of the body had not been established as a plain fact. No one could produce the dead body, and no one has ever put forward a satisfactory explanation for this. Clearly the *disciples* did not steal the body, for many of them died afterwards for their belief that Christ was risen. Would they have suffered martyrdom for what they knew was a lie? The *Romans* were not guilty, for they were plainly embarrassed that the body had disappeared when the tomb had been sealed and guarded by soldiers. If the *Jews* had stolen the body, they would at once have produced it to silence the preaching of the risen Christ once for all. There is only one satisfactory solution to the puzzle: Christ rose from the dead!

Fourth, there were many resurrection appearances,

and the risen Christ was seen over a period of six weeks on eleven different occasions by at least 550 people, many of whom were still alive when the evidence was recorded in the New Testament documents; and no one has ever tried to dispute this.

Fifth, we have the testimony of millions of Christians over 2,000 years who have known that Jesus is real and alive in their own experience. Some of these have come from other faiths; some from atheism and humanism; some from a purely nominal Christian faith. There are many today who are willing to die for what they know to be true concerning the living Christ, and it is sobering to realise that there have probably been more Christian martyrs during this century than during the rest of the history of the Christian church put together.

Consequences

In the light of the resurrection of Christ, there are a number of important consequences.

In the first place, the death of Christ was not a tragedy but a triumph. All the disciples were filled with gloom at the time of the crucifixion. To them Christ's sufferings and death seemed a senseless end to a glorious life. What a tragedy! Why had God allowed it? That question was answered after the resurrection. God in Christ had dealt with the problem of sin once for all. The penalty had been paid. When Jesus cried out 'It is finished!', it was not a cry of total despair, as the disciples had first thought. It was a triumphant shout: 'Finished! Accomplished!' The single Greek word was sometimes stamped across bills that had been paid. PAID! That is what Jesus accomplished through his death. 'There is no condemnation now for those who live in union with Christ Jesus.' (Romans 8:1 (TEV)) And he rose again to show us that this is true.

In the second place, the victory of Christ over Satan and all the powers of evil is complete. Paul once wrote that because of the death of Christ on the cross, God has 'disarmed the principalities and powers.' (Colossians

2 : 15) He has not yet annihilated them. They are still active; they can and do cause much trouble. But like a defeated army, humiliated, captured and stripped of weapons, they are powerless against Jesus Christ and his followers.

On one university mission a young man asked if he could see me, and we fixed a time the next day. Unexpectedly he brought a girl with him. As she entered the room I had an overpowering sense of evil which filled me with sudden fear. I quietly claimed the authority and victory of Jesus over this, and the fear vanished as quickly as it had come. We then talked; and it transpired that the girl was a practising medium, steeped in occult practices. I had no previous knowledge of this – just this sudden, powerful sense of evil. But I had also experienced the greater power of Christ! Through the death and resurrection of Christ, a Christian has nothing whatever to fear when faced with evil forces, providing he is trusting in Christ's authority and protection.

In the third place, because of the resurrection we know that there is a life after death. Although we cannot know the precise details, since they are outside our present total experience, we do know that this life will be unimaginably wonderful for those who love Christ. A true Christian, filled with the Spirit, will at times know something of the indescribable joy of being totally caught up in the presence of Christ. But the consummation of our relationship with Christ will be so glorious, and so beyond our present experience, that the Bible often describes it in negatives. In heaven there will be no sin, no evil, no fears, no decay, no pollution, no suffering, no loneliness, no hunger, no thirst, no sorrow: 'God will wipe away every tear from their eyes.' (Revelation 7 : 15–17; see also Revelation 21–22)

Thus, for the Christian there is nothing whatever to fear in the face of death. 'I am the resurrection and the life,' said Jesus. 'Whoever believes in me will live, even though he dies.' (John 11 : 25 (TEV)) And he rose again to show that he had the right to make such a devastating claim.

In the fourth place, however, Christ's resurrection demonstrates the truth about judgement. Jesus is Lord; and one day, at the name of Jesus every knee shall bow and every tongue shall confess that Jesus Christ is Lord. (Philippians 2: 10f) Further, unless we bow to him as our Lord and Saviour we shall *have* to bow to him one day as our Lord and Judge.

There is a legend about a man caught in the quicksands. It is no doubt a caricature, but most caricatures contain a good element of the truth. Here was this man struggling and passing rapidly to his death. Confucius saw him and remarked, 'There is evidence that men should stay out of such places.' Buddha came and said, 'Let that life be a lesson to the rest of the world.' Mohammed commented, 'Alas! It is the will of Allah!' A Hindu said, 'Never mind, you will return to earth in another form.' But when Jesus saw him he said, 'Give me your hand, brother, and I will pull you out.' We are all caught in the quicksand of death. We cannot escape it. Neither Confucius, Buddha, Mohammed nor anyone else can help us or save us. At best we have their teachings and writings. Only Jesus is alive. Therefore, only Jesus can stretch out a hand and take you into the presence of the living God forever. No wonder Paul, having considered carefully the truth of the resurrection of Christ, once cried out, 'Thanks be to God who gives us the victory through our Lord Jesus Christ!' (1 Corinthians 15: 27)

7
Open to Life

The morning service had just finished in Washington Cathedral, and the congregation were coming to greet their English guest preacher, who happened to be me! 'Could I see you sometime?' asked a young man, who had obviously been stirred by something in the sermon.

Later that day Richard and I were deep in conversation. Richard was obviously gifted and intelligent, the son of a Judge, and himself a law student at the University of Virginia. He was at that time doing a vacation job – a cab driver in the city of Washington, DC.

At the end of a long but extremely valuable conversation, when I sensed that the Spirit of God was working quietly but deeply in Richard's life, we knelt and prayed. Very simply Richard asked Jesus Christ to become his Lord and Saviour and to enter his life by his Holy Spirit.

Before we parted I explained that there might be no sudden or dramatic experience, but that increasingly he would know the reality of Christ as he sought to deepen this new-found relationship, and I gave him a little guidance about this. I had no further contact or correspondence with Richard until he wrote to me three months later.

'It took me a few weeks to realize it but the fact is that something has been very different about my whole life since my conversion; I still can't describe exactly what the difference is. There is a tremendous sense of a load off my shoulders, of an end of running around "like a chicken with his head chopped off," of relief in general, of joy, peace and happiness, but those words only begin to do the job. There is an absolute certainty of the presence in my life of an Individual who cares about me more than I could ever care about anyone else; who knows and shares my every thought, joy or care; of whom I can ask anything; and who is always, always there. It is too good to be true, or so it would seem, and yet it is as real as night and day.'

Richard, of course, is only one of hundreds of thousands who can speak of the same transformation in their life. The individuals concerned may be of different ages, from different backgrounds, education, culture, race and colour, and yet there is one obvious common factor. They all speak of a new life in Jesus Christ. I am not saying that they never had any doubts or problems, but increasingly they know that something radical has happened which concerns the whole of their life. It is the Spirit of God that has come to live within them as they put their trust in Christ. Without this fact, there would be no Christian Church at all. Indeed, the whole spiritual revolution that Christ inaugurated would have died a natural death in the first century.

During the earthly ministry of Jesus, his disciples were wholly dependent on him. Without him they were often faithless, fearful and foolish. Frequently Jesus had to say to them, 'O you of little faith!', 'Have you no faith?', 'Why did you doubt?' Often they missed the point altogether. Sometimes they failed miserably. And at the supreme test, with the events leading up to the crucifixion, one betrayed Jesus, another denied him, and all deserted him when the going proved too tough. This was not very promising material for the start of the greatest revolution the world has ever seen. Moreover, just before Christ's ascension into heaven, his disciples asked him when he would finish the job for them. When would he throw out the Roman occupation and

restore the kingdom to Israel? This is how he replied:
'You will be filled with power when the Holy Spirit
comes on you; and you will be witnesses for me in
Jerusalem, in all of Judea and Samaria, and to the ends
of the earth.' (Acts 1 : 8 (TEV)) A moment later he left
them – for good.

Of course, they felt utterly helpless and very frightened. They huddled behind locked doors for fear of
the Jews. They had no power and no wish to witness to
Jesus, especially in Jerusalem where their Master had
been so recently murdered. All they could possibly do
was to hold on to this promise of the Spirit of God. And
it is simply a historical fact that something very remarkable happened. These ordinary, timid disciples were
filled with a new life and a new confidence that they
had never known before. They were possessed with a
love and a joy and a power which gave them immense
boldness and authority wherever they went. Many
thousands found the living Christ; the sick were healed;
signs and wonders took place in the name of Jesus. They
were opposed, beaten, imprisoned, killed. But on and
on they went. As J B Phillips expressed it in his preface
to the Acts of the Apostles, 'It is a matter of sober historical fact that never before has any small body of
ordinary people so moved the world that their enemies
could say with tears of rage in their eyes that these men
have turned the world upside down!'

What has brought about this change? There was no
dynamic leader, no successor to Jesus Christ. It was the
promised Holy Spirit who had come to dwell in the life
of every true believer in Christ. Paul once wrote, 'When
someone becomes a Christian he becomes a brand new
person inside. He is not the same any more. A new life
has begun!' (2 Corinthians 5: 17 (Living Bible))

How else can you explain historical facts like these?
What other explanation can there be for the birth and
growth of the Christian church, from tiny and timid
beginnings? What of the testimonies of millions of
people right up to the present day who speak of this

new life? It is true that the record of the Church, as an *institution*, has been very mixed. No one can defend, on Christian terms, the religious wars or persecutions, the pseudo-religious conflict in Northern Ireland, or the hypocrisies and inconsistencies of the Church which drove Karl Marx to Communism and Sigmund Freud to psycho-analysis. It is all too obvious why some have been driven away from a vital faith in Christ because of the obstacle of the Church. However, it is important to remember two truths. First, religion and true Christianity can be two very different things. It was religious people who most of all opposed Christ and finally crucified him. And religion has frequently been the enemy of the real thing – the devil's counterfeit. Secondly, even within the true Christian Church, Christ said there would always be both wheat and tares, both the good and the bad, which would not be separated until the final day of judgement. The best definition of the Church I know is that it is 'Christ's hospital.' If I visit a hospital which claims to heal sick people, and find it full of sick people, I do not say 'What a wretched hospital! What hypocrisy!' Instead, I am glad to know that it is in touch with the right people. Likewise the Church is a fellowship of sinners. If its members are still morally and spiritually sick in various degrees, it is not a denial of the truth of the Christian faith, but only that the Church is in touch with the right people. Indeed, it is part of the evidence of the Holy Spirit that he can take such very ordinary, selfish, sinful human beings, and do so much *in* them and *through* them as he has done all down the centuries. It is part of the reality of the Spirit that the Church, in spite of all its numerous faults and failings, still exists, and in some parts of the world is expanding more rapidly than the exploding birth-rate itself.

Let us look further at this new life brought to us by the Holy Spirit as we put our trust in Jesus Christ; drawing our thoughts mainly from one of the great chapters in the Bible on the Spirit's work – Romans 8.

The Spirit sets us free from all that spoils life

'For the law of the Spirit of life in Christ Jesus has set me free from the law of sin and death.' (Romans 8: 2) In the first seven chapters of Romans, Paul has been expounding on man's situation in the sight of God. Everyone can know something about God: his reality and power have been clearly revealed in the things that have been made. We see the evidence of God in the design and wonder of creation all around us. Further, God's laws and moral standards are also known, to some extent at least, by our conscience even if we are totally ignorant of God's self-revelation in the Bible and in his Son, Jesus Christ. However, the truth is this: whatever knowledge of God's laws we may or may not have had, we have all fallen far short of his perfect standards, or even of our own imperfect standards. Therefore we have all sinned in God's eyes and desperately need to be forgiven and to be made right with God.

In Romans 5, Paul uses four words to describe our situation. We are *helpless* and cannot live as God wants us to live; we are *ungodly* and do not put God at the centre of our lives where he ought to be; we are *sinners* because we break God's commandments; we are *enemies* and go our own way, not God's way; we do what we want, not what God wants. Alongside those four words Paul puts one fact:

> *While we were yet helpless* Christ died.
> Christ died *for the ungodly.*
> *While we were yet sinners* Christ died.
> *While we were enemies we were reconciled to God by the* death of his Son.

Four times, therefore, Paul puts the cross of Christ as the answer to man's supreme problem, sin. Elsewhere in the New Testament the truth shines out as clearly as can be. 'Now in Christ Jesus you who were once far off have been brought near in the blood of Christ.' (Ephesians 2: 13) 'We have confidence to enter the sanctuary (= God's presence) by the blood of Jesus.' (Hebrews 10: 19) 'Christ also died for sins once for all, the righteous for the unrighteous, that he might bring us to God.' (1 Peter 3: 18) No one can find God or come to God except through the blood of God's own Son Jesus Christ. This is our only hope of reconciliation. But having come to God through Jesus we still need something more.

The humanist Walter Lippman made this perceptive comment after the last world war, 'We ourselves were so sure that at long last a generation had arisen, keen and eager to put this disorderly earth to right ... and fit to do it.... We meant so well, we tried so hard, and look what we have made of it. We can only muddle into muddle. What is required is a new kind of man.'

It is because of this that God offers us not only a Saviour to take away the guilt of the past, but also his Spirit to transform our lives here and now. You see, the things that spoil our lives most of all – and the lives of others too – are not the things around us but the things within us.

It is, then, from within, out of the very heart of man, that all the problems spring. (Mark 7: 21–23) These are the things that pull us down; my selfishness, my greed, my self-pity, my resentment. And the trouble is that, when we try to overcome these problems ourselves, we find that we simply cannot do it. Paul expresses this frustration in vivid terms: 'For I know that nothing good dwells within me, that is, in my flesh. I can will what is right, but I cannot do it. For I do not do the good I want, but the evil I do not want is what I do.... Wretched man that I am! Who will deliver me from this body of death?' (Romans 7: 18, 19, 24) Then after this cry of despair we find a sudden burst of praise and freedom in the next breath: 'For the law of the Spirit of life in Christ Jesus has set me free from the law of sin and death.' (Romans 8: 2)

How can Paul swing so suddenly from one experience to the other? The key to it all is this: in the last depressing ten verses of Romans 7 Paul mentions 'I' twenty-five times and 'me' or 'my' thirteen times. Here we have thirty-eight references to himself in ten verses! And the Holy Spirit is not mentioned once. But in Romans 8 the Holy Spirit is mentioned nineteen times with 'I' only twice. Therefore it is the Holy Spirit who sets us free from all that spoils our lives. Naturally the law of sin and death brings us down; but the Spirit of life in Christ Jesus not only overcomes the downward pull of sin and death but lifts us up into a new quality of life altogether. It is the self-life that is responsible for all those attitudes and actions that cause such misery: 'immorality, impurity, licentiousness, idolatry, sorcery, enmity, strife, jealousy, anger, selfishness, dissension, party spirit, envy, drunkenness, carousing, and the like.' (Galatians 5 : 19–21) However, the Spirit's life is gloriously different: 'Love, joy, peace, patience, kindness, goodness, faithfulness, gentleness, self-control.' (Galatians 5 : 22f) And that transformation is not only a fact in human experience, but it is perhaps the greatest miracle that we could ever witness. The Jewish philosopher, Martin Buber, once asked, 'Is there any force in the world that can change that intractable thing, human nature? There's a tragedy at the heart of things.' There is no force in the world that can change the heart of man; it is only the Spirit of Jesus who can make us into his likeness. One woman changed so much when she met with Christ that she thought it best to send a new photograph to be attached to her passport. But even she was surprised when an official from the passport office rang to say that it was impossible to stick the new photo beside the old one because it looked like an entirely different person. He told her that she must now apply for a new passport, with signatures to confirm that it really was the same person! (Told by Basilea Schlink in *You Will Never be the Same* (Marshall, Morgan & Scott))

No one is claiming for a moment that a Christian is perfect. In fact, it is perhaps only the Christian who realises just how imperfect he really is. All the great men and women of God have been deeply conscious of their own faults and failings, and have longed to be more like Jesus. John Newton once summed it up neatly like this: 'I am not what I ought to be; I am not what I would like to be; I am not what I hope to be. But I am not what I was; and by the grace of God I am what I am.'

Moreover when a person is increasingly full of an unusually rich quality of love, joy and peace, then that person knows something of real wealth. The whole world is often crazy in search of these things, but they come to us in the fullest and richest sense when the Spirit of God comes to dwell within us. As one woman wrote to me, 'I have had many joys in my life, but the most wonderful joy of them all is the re-birth in Jesus Christ. It's made a tremendous difference; the love of Jesus is always there – new and fresh every morning.'

The Spirit sets us free to enjoy God

In Paul's words, 'The old sinful nature within us is against God.... It can never please God. But you are not like that. You are controlled by your new nature if you have the Spirit of God living in you.' (Romans 8:7–9 (Living Bible))

I have always loved the question asked in the Scottish Catechism: 'What is the chief end of man?' It is the question that people are asking all over the world at this moment. The answer is: 'To glorify God and to enjoy him forever.' How far do you *enjoy* God? Is he a real person in your life? Does he fill you with such a quality of life and joy that you could never find anywhere else? The purpose of life is not to have an academic discussion about the possibility of God's existence. It is to enjoy him, to know him, to love him and to experience his love in our own lives. That is the chief end of man! Jesus said exactly the same thing: eternal life, the life for which God created and made us, is summed up in knowing God and knowing Jesus Christ.

(John 17 : 3) Therefore we have not opened up to life until we have opened up to God. Indeed it is something so significantly and fundamentally new that Jesus called it a new birth, a spiritual birth which is essential before we can come to know God, since God is Spirit.

When a thoroughly respectable and religious man came to Jesus one night because he was interested in this unusual preacher, Jesus said to him, in effect, three things: 'You must be born again! You must be born again! You must be born again!' He said it three times. Why? Because unless a man is born again he cannot see the Kingdom of God – he is blind to it – and he cannot enter the Kingdom of God – he is dead to it. Therefore, it is imperative that each person must be born again before he can come into God's presence and kingdom (see John 3 : 1–7). A Rector of a large and prosperous church, the Reverend Charles Jarman who held several university degrees in theology, said this: 'I preached for 52 years before I knew the Lord Jesus as my personal Saviour! True I was a minister, and thought I was a Christian, but that did not make me one.' And in the story of his life he recorded how on March 28th, 1966, he knelt down and for the first time asked Christ to come into his life. 'I have never felt such peace.... I knew that I was born again in Christ Jesus.'

It does not matter who a person is, bishop, minister, theologian, respectable agnostic, militant atheist, faithful churchgoer. Unless that person is born again by the Spirit of God he can neither see nor enter the Kingdom of God. So said the Son of God! Of course it is tragic if a person shows no interest in this new birth. God longs that each of us should enjoy him – not discuss him, nor debate him, nor argue about him but simply enjoy him.

There are simply countless Christians all over the world whose lives could speak eloquently of the joy that Jesus brings. One student told me, with her eyes sparkling with life, of the 'incredible joy of the Holy Spirit, a joy bubbling up inside her.'

The Spirit sets us free to pray to God

'Those who are led by God's Spirit are God's sons. For the Spirit that God has given you does not make you a slave and cause you to be afraid; instead, the Spirit makes you God's sons, and by the Spirit's power we cry to God, "Father! my Father!"' (Romans 8:14-16 (TEV))

The Spirit, therefore, helps us to enjoy God, not only in terms of the high spots when there is a great time of worship and praise with other Christians, or when we may have special spiritual experiences, but in developing our whole relationship with God so that something deep down within us wants to cry out 'Abba! Father!'

Often there are two fears about a personal commitment to Christ. First there is a fear that there may be a very sudden change so that we are perfectly normal one day and super-religious the next! The truth is, of course, that it very seldom happens like that. Although there is a new birth which is both decisive and wonderful, it is a new birth leading to a new relationship; and very few relationships explode overnight. Normally they develop gradually. Certainly there may be some things which need to be put right at once; but other changes will occur slowly but surely as the friendship with Jesus becomes more real and personal. This may have the effect of making some other pursuits in life hollow and superficial in comparison.

The second fear is, 'I could never keep it up.' The answer is that in our own strength that is true. But the Spirit of God comes to live within us, helping us to do the very things that we could not do ourselves. Paul says, 'The Spirit helps us in our weakness.' In particular he helps us to develop our relationship with God. He helps us to understand the Bible, so that we begin to see how God can speak to us day by day. He helps us to pray, so that quite naturally we begin to talk to God and share our life with him and let him share his life with us. The Spirit helps us to overcome some of the sins in our lives, changing our selfishness into love, our pride into humility, our greed into generosity. The Spirit helps us to know God, to live for God, to bring the reality of God to other people, to love other people. There is not an area in our life that the Holy Spirit cannot enrich with his presence and power. Certainly Jesus wants to be Lord of our lives, otherwise he cannot transform our lives according to his best plan for us. But in every way he helps us to fulfil that plan by his Spirit. As a seed planted in the ground grows up into something beautiful and fragrant, so the Holy Spirit within us, planted in our hearts when we respond personally to Jesus, begins a process which develops into a beautiful personal relationship with the living God.

The Spirit sets us free from all fear

Fear can be an extraordinarily powerful factor in our lives. We may be afraid of other people, afraid of what they may think or say about us. Perhaps we are afraid of our future, or of pain, sickness or death. Well, the promise of Paul is clear: 'For we know that in all things God works for good with those who love him, those whom he has called according to his purpose. . . . If God is for us who can be against us? He did not even keep back his own Son, but offered him for us all! He gave us his Son – will he not also freely give us all things? . . . For I am certain that nothing can separate us from his love: neither death nor life; neither angels nor other heavenly rulers or powers; neither the present nor the future, neither the world above or the world below – there is nothing in all creation that will ever be able to separate us from the love of God which is ours through Christ Jesus our Lord.' (Romans 8:28, 31–32, 38–39 (TEV))

One summer I met a lovely American girl who had a little baby. Her husband was in the Military and on a particularly dangerous mission in Vietnam. She told me how she had been full of fear, for him, for her baby, and for herself. Then God gave her the faith to believe these promises from Romans 8, and it was perfectly obvious to me that she was filled with God's peace.

The Christian knows, through the death and resurrection of Jesus, that even when death does come we are not separated from God's love. We are simply more fully and perfectly in God's presence than ever before. On Martin Luther King's memorial are these simple words:

REVEREND MARTIN LUTHER KING, JUNIOR
1929–1968
'FREE AT LAST, FREE AT LAST,
THANK GOD A'MIGHTY,
I AM FREE AT LAST'

8
Why Bother?

Apathy rules the day! 'Yes, I am interested in the Christian faith. Perhaps there is a God. Maybe Jesus is alive. I'll think about it – sometime.' The majority of people today are neither for Christ nor against Christ. They may be interested; they may be impressed; they may be in search of God; but they do not want to get personally involved with Christ and with the Christian faith.

In this chapter, let us focus attention on one man who had to make up his mind about Jesus: Pontius Pilate, Roman governor of Judea. He tried very hard to remain neutral, and did not want to be personally involved with the intriguing yet puzzling figure of Jesus. He was frankly disturbed when Jesus was brought as a prisoner before him; and, although he struggled first of all with the crowd and then with his own conscience, he tried to wash his hands of the whole business. 'When Pilate saw that he was gaining nothing, but rather that a riot was beginning, he took water and washed his hands before the crowd, saying "I am innocent of this man's blood: see to it yourselves." ' (Matthew 27:24)

However, concerning the great issues of life and death, God and man, there is no neutral position at all. These are issues which inevitably affect every single one of us. We cannot remain uninvolved. Christ spoke with immense authority about the meaning and purpose of life, about death and what happens after death, about the nature of man and the nature of God, about the need of man in the sight of God, about sin, forgiveness, love and peace. And concerning these issues, with many others like them, there can be no neutral position because these are entwined in our very life and death. We may refuse to make up our minds on these matters but we cannot refuse to make up our life. Our life is being made up in one direction or another all the time.

The Nationalist Chinese Foreign Minister at the United Nations General Assembly in 1961 quoted the following definition from the Peking New Terminology Dictionary: '*Neutralist line:* a daydream that can never be realized. Even its theory is not correct. There are only two roads, either to support capitalism or to support socialism. There is no third road. Any vain hope to take on a third road is doomed to failure.' A Christian dictionary might have a very similar definition: '*Neutralist line:* a daydream that can never be realized. Even its theory is not correct. There are only two roads, one leading to life and the other leading to destruction. There is no third road. Any vain hope to take on a third road is doomed to failure.'

Why then do people doubt? Why are so few willing to get personally involved with Christ? Let us look more carefully at Pontius Pilate. Basically, there were two reasons why he tried so hard to remain neutral.

He was not sure about Christ

At least he was not 100% sure. There were some questions he just could not answer. The more he studied Christ, the more he was puzzled and mystified. 'Now Jesus stood before the governor; and the governor asked him, "Are you the King of the Jews?" Jesus said to him, "You have said so." But when he was accused by the chief priests and elders, he made no answer. Then Pilate said to him, "Do you not hear how many things they testify against you?' But he gave him no answer not even to a single charge; so that the governor wondered greatly.' (Matthew 27: 11–14)

Many today also are confused and unsure about Christ. And they want to be completely and absolutely sure before they are prepared to act. Nevertheless, in my experience, there are many reasons for doubt. Let me give some of them.

1 Prejudice

A student once said to me, 'I've made up my mind; don't confuse me with facts!' Most of us are creatures of prejudice to some extent. I can understand a person who has been disillusioned by what may seem to be stuffy, established, church-ianity. The vital thing, however, is to be open and honest, and willing to change your mind. There is nothing so deadly as a closed mind.

There was a man who once thought that he was dead. Nothing that his parents, doctors, friends or psychiatrists could do could persuade him otherwise. One psychiatrist, however, worked out a plan of action. After studying together a medical textbook, he managed to convince the man of one simple fact: dead men do not bleed. 'Yes, I agree,' said the man, 'dead men do not bleed!' Whereupon the psychiatrist plunged a small knife into the man's arm and the blood started to flow. The man looked at his arm, his face white with astonishment and horror. 'Goodness me!' he said. 'Dead men bleed after all!'

Now in one sense that man was already dead, because he was not alive to reality; he was unable to change his mind. And many today are spiritually dead in that they will not consider the possibility that Christ might be right and they might be wrong. Prejudice is a most destructive and dangerous thing.

2 Insufficient evidence

I was having breakfast in an Oxford College a few years ago, with an intelligent lawyer sitting opposite me. Having discovered I was a clergyman (for I was in disguise), he said, 'I'm an atheist. What are you going to do with me?' I replied, 'As a lawyer you will appreciate the need to consider the evidence carefully before coming to any verdict. Have you considered the evidence for Jesus Christ?' It was soon transparently clear that he was very largely ignorant of the evidence of Christ, and had more or less dismissed the Christian faith on purely superficial grounds. He knew almost nothing about the historical reliability of the New Testament documents, the solid substantial evidence of the person of Christ or the resurrection of Christ, the facts relating to the formation of the Christian Church, and the personal experience of countless millions of Christians all down the centuries.

This is tragic. Jesus said that our response to him was of total importance, affecting both our life and the whole of eternity. The meaning of our present existence depends on our relationship with him. What happens at death depends upon our response to him. Questions of forgiveness, peace and hope are all wrapped up in him. If that is not true, forget it! But if it is true, the person and teaching of Jesus must radically affect every single one of us. At the very least we ought to examine the evidence as carefully as possible. And if we do that, it is certainly powerful enough to take a rational step of faith.

3 No sense of need

'I am perfectly all right as I am; I don't need a god crutch.' The real question, of course, is not 'Do I feel a need?' but 'Is it true?' In the physical realm it is possible to suffer from euphoria: you may feel astonishingly well yet in fact you are sick. There is also spiritual euphoria. This is what Jesus made so clear. And the one person with the qualifications to speak about our need before God kept on saying that, whether we feel it or not, we have a tremendous need, so great that he was willing to die for us on the cross to make it possible for us to be forgiven.

For example, look at the commandments of God. It is not what I think about God that matters; it is what God thinks about me that really counts. And he has given us very clear instructions and commandments. Let me put the Ten Commandments in the form of questions. Have you always put God first in your life where he ought to be? Have you ever put anything in the place of God in your life? Have you ever taken his name, or the name of Jesus carelessly on your lips? Have you always kept one day a week for worship and rest? Have you always respected and honoured your parents? Have you never hated anyone, never become bitter, resentful? Have you never had sex outside marriage, never harboured impure thoughts or lusts and desires? Have you never stolen, not ever a person's reputation? Have you never told a lie or half-truth about another person? Have you never coveted what is not yours? Covetousness is perhaps the major sin of today. If you have ever failed in any of those points, then you are guilty before God, under his judgement, and in desperate need of his forgiveness. If that were not true, said Paul, Christ died for nothing!

Therefore it is not a question of feeling a need, but of being humble enough to listen to Christ, to hear what he says and see what he did, supremely on the cross. 'I am the way ... no one comes to the Father but by me.' A person is free to ignore him if he wants to; but he is not free to ignore the consequences.

4 Once bitten, twice shy

'I've tried before, but it hasn't worked.' If that is so I can understand a person's hesitation, but let me say three things about this. In the first place, did you really begin a personal *relationship* with Jesus? I was confirmed 11 years before taking that step. I had tried, I had turned over a new leaf; but how different it was when I found a new life.

In the second place, did you go on to *deepen* that relationship with Jesus? All relationships must be developed. Most relationships do not blossom overnight, and they need to be worked at. As soon as we take any relationship for granted, that is the start of trouble.

In the third place, do not try to analyse too precisely what may have happened in the past. Perhaps you have already committed your life 'in pencil' years ago. Well now, ink it over. God wants you to be quite sure about your relationship with him.

5 Fear

A brilliant young barrister openly admitted what was holding him back from a personal commitment to Christ. 'It is the fear of getting involved.' Many people know this: a fear that Christ might upset their social life, their ambitions, or their plans. A fear of losing a few friends, a fear of what their friends might say, a fear of being laughed at.

Fortunately Jesus was not afraid of those things. For our sake, to take away the guilt of our sin, he was willing to be 'despised and rejected by men, a man of sorrows and acquainted with grief.' He was willing to be 'wounded for our transgressions, bruised for our iniquities.' He was willing to be 'oppressed, stricken, afflicted.' He became the sacrificial offering for our sins as the Lord laid on him the guilt of us all (see Isaiah 53). If ever we are afraid of getting involved, we need to look carefully at the cross of Jesus Christ. Our fears, frankly, are a pathetic mixture of pride, self-centredness, and short-sightedness. Jesus, in his love, gave us many, many warnings of the judgement to come if we try to remain neutral. 'What does it profit a man to gain the whole world and forfeit his life?' (Mark 8: 36) 'On that day many will say to me "Lord, Lord did we not ... do many mighty works in your name?' and then will I declare to them, 'I never knew you; depart from me. ..."' (Matthew 7: 22f) So much of his teaching contains realistic warnings as to what will happen if we choose to ignore or reject him.

Of course, it is a very poor thing if we turn to Christ only because we are afraid of the judgement. But such is the love and humility of God that he is willing to accept us even on those terms. Therefore he is willing, in his love, to warn us of the folly of neglect. He longs that we might know his love and friendship in our own experience.

Coming back to Pontius Pilate, I do not think he was really so unsure about Christ. He knew perfectly well, for example, that Christ was innocent. There was almost certainly another reason which made Pilate determined to remain neutral if at all possible.

He was not willing to get involved
There were probably two reasons at least for this.

In the first place he was swayed by the crowd. On that first Good Friday, being the time of the feast of the Passover, it was the custom of the governor to release one prisoner. One half of him wanted very much to release Jesus. 'He asked them, "Do you want me to release for you the King of the Jews?" For he perceived that it was out of envy that the chief priests had delivered him up. But the chief priests stirred up the crowd to have him release for them Barabbas instead. And Pilate again said to them, "Then what shall I do with the man whom you call the King of the Jews?" And they cried out again, "Crucify him." And Pilate said to them, "Why, what evil has he done?" But they shouted all the more, "Crucify him." So Pilate, wishing to satisfy the crowd, released for them Barabbas; and having scourged Jesus, he delivered him to be crucified.' (Mark 15 : 9–15)

There we have it: *wishing to satisfy the crowd.* Many have the same pull in their lives. What we may not realize is that some of our 'crowd,' however self-confident or rebellious they may appear on the surface, are probably deep-down hungry for God or for some kind of spiritual reality. How foolish if we hold back because of our friends!

In the second place there was personal ambition. The Jewish ringleaders suddenly threw down their trump card! 'If you release this man, you are not Caesar's friend!' That did it! At once Jesus was sent to the cross.

The question is, How successfully did Pilate remain neutral and uninvolved? In one sense the answer is obvious. For 2,000 years millions of Christians have said each week in the Apostles' Creed, 'Jesus Christ crucified under Pontius Pilate.' There is no neutral position.

More than that, Pilate suffered later from a bad conscience. According to Greek historians, shortly after this incident he committed suicide in Rome. No doubt there were other reasons as well, but no one can finally silence his conscience.

Further, Pilate missed the whole truth about life, even though it was there right in front of him. 'What is truth?' he asked rhetorically. And there was Jesus standing before him, the man who had said 'I am the truth.' But Pilate missed it.

One further step

So far in our search for God we have looked at some of the evidence for God's self-revelation in his Son. We have looked at Jesus yesterday, seeing something of the historical facts of his person, his death and his resurrection, and the development of the Christian Church. We have looked at Jesus today, seeing his reality in the lives of many different people from many different backgrounds. However, there is still one final piece of evidence that anyone can have, and indeed must have, when they have done all the reading, talking and thinking in the world. You can discover the reality of God when you come to know Jesus for yourself, when you sincerely ask him to come into your life. Nothing that I could say, or anyone else could say, could be a substitute for that.

One young person at a special service asked Christ to come into her life. Six weeks later she wrote to me to say how very real it had all become in her experience. Then she said this in her letter, 'I'd been thinking carefully, but warily, about Christianity for a long time. ... That evening was a great step forward because for the first time I felt truly involved in the whole experience of finding Christ. Previously I had argued intellectually from a distance, but although I was becoming more and more convinced that Jesus had all the answers, I still did not feel near to the heart of it all.... Now I realize that no matter how much arguing is done about the historical evidence for Jesus, etc., *the only answer is to enter into a personal relationship with Jesus himself,* and then he will help you and will answer your questions.' That is the heart of it all. A person may talk for 3,000 years and still go round and round in circles. 'The only answer is to enter into a personal relationship with Jesus himself.' This is the most important thing we can do in our life. Without this we have no God, no hope, nothing of ultimate value.

How, then, can we become personally involved?

9
Finding God

To one genuine seeker Jesus said, 'Zacchaeus, hurry up and come down. I must be your guest today!' (Luke 19:5ff (J B Phillips)) So Zacchaeus, who from a mixture of fascination and fear was hiding in a sycamore tree, 'hurriedly climbed down and gladly welcomed him.'

How many of us are like Zacchaeus! One half of us wants to know the truth about God and longs for Jesus to become real and personal in our lives. We see the evidence and we talk with friends who have found him. And yet we are afraid. What will others say? What will Jesus do? How much will my life have to change? Am I losing my independence? There's too much to give up!

Most of us know this tug-of-war inside us.

Jesus today

One thing is clear. When Jesus calls us by name (and in our heart or conscience we seem to know deep down when that is so) there is some urgency about it. 'Hurry up!' he says. 'I must be your guest *today*!' Jesus is *today's* man.

God's time is therefore always today, and the Scriptures frequently make this clear: – 'Today, when you hear his voice, do not harden your hearts' (Psalm 95:7) – 'Now is the acceptable time ... now is the day of salvation' (2 Corinthians 6:2) – 'Seek the Lord while he may be found, call upon him while he is near.' (Isaiah 55 : 6)

How then can we welcome Jesus into the house of our life? Four words may clarify the steps that we need to take: Turn, Trust, Take and Thank.

1 Turn

If I realize that I have been going my own way through life, I must be willing to turn right round and go with Jesus. This is what the Bible calls repentance. Repentance means much more than being sorry for sin. Feeling sorry can all too easily spring from self-pity. Rather, I must humbly admit that I have broken God's laws, rebelled against him, hurt him, and displeased him; and now I am willing to turn right away from all that I know is wrong in my life. If I am willing to do that, and to turn round to Jesus, taking him with both hands, then I have taken the first vital step. Zacchaeus, the well-known cheat and swindler, said to Jesus, 'Look, sir, I will give half my property to the poor. And if I have swindled anybody out of anything I will pay him back four times as much.'

Don't worry if you are not yet sure of all the wrong things in your life. God, in his gentleness, shows us our wrongdoings step by step. But you cannot hold on to what you *know* is wrong in one hand, and try to take Jesus with the other. It simply does not work. Jesus is not interested in compromise – any more than a dentist is happy to leave four bad teeth in your mouth just because you asked him to deal only with the one that hurts!

2 Trust

I must trust Jesus in two ways. First, I must trust him as my *Saviour*, who had taken all my sin upon himself when he died on the Cross. This is the only way I could ever come into God's presence. And, wonderfully, Christ has paid the penalty for all my sin; there is nothing for me to pay.

Secondly, I must trust Jesus as my *Lord*, inviting him into my life, not only as Guest, but as Master and Owner. Every part of my life must now come under his control: my plans and ambitions, my business life and social life, my study and sport, my home and family, girl-friend or boy-friend, husband or wife. And I must trust him as Lord of all these things because he alone always knows what is best. He never comes to spoil my life – only to enrich it. He cares about my well-being more than anyone ever could. Therefore he must take control as Lord of all.

3 Take

'The free gift of God is eternal life in Christ Jesus our Lord.' (Romans 6:23) Although God offers me this priceless gift – the gift of his own Son – if I do not take it, I will not have it. It is tragically as simple as that. God will not throw his gifts at me, whether I want them or not.

He just waits for me to stretch out my empty hands and take from him this most valuable gift that I could ever have, the gift of eternal life in Jesus Christ.

In practice how do I take it, or take *him*? Zacchaeus simply 'welcomed' Jesus into his house; and Jesus said, 'Salvation has come to this house today!'

A famous promise of Jesus is in Revelation 3:20. 'Behold, I stand at the door and knock; if anyone hears my voice and opens the door, I will come in to him. . . .' The picture is quite clear. If you are sitting at home waiting for a friend to arrive, and suddenly you hear a knock, what do you do? Of course you open the door; and if it is your friend, you say 'Come in!' You have now welcomed him into your house.

So it is with Jesus: In a simple prayer I must ask him to come into my life. And as soon as I do that and mean it, then I receive Jesus – or more accurately, I receive the Spirit of Jesus, the Holy Spirit – into my life. A new relationship with God, Father, Son and Spirit, has now begun.

4 Thank

The essence of all relationships is faith, and faith means taking a person at his word. No relationship would be possible if I did not believe a person's word. Again, so it is with Jesus. Whether or not I feel anything when I ask Jesus to come in, I must believe that he *has* come in, because that is his solemn word. Therefore, in faith, I say 'Thank you!' As with so many aspects in life, it is only when we *act* as though something were true that it ever becomes true. For example, it is only when I take a cheque to my bank that it will ever become true in my account!

With Jesus, then, I must believe his promise, thank him that he is now in my life (having invited him), and begin to act as though it were true. It *is* true, and it will wonderfully become true in my experience. 'Whatever you ask in prayer,' said Jesus, 'believe that you receive it, *and you will*.' (Mark 11 : 24)

Have you ever personally asked Jesus into your life? Are you quite sure? Are you sure that he is now with you? Is God real in your experience? If the answer to any of those questions is 'No,' then you could pray a very simple prayer now, quietly and simply, wherever you are. If possible, of course, get alone somewhere, and many people find it helpful to kneel when they pray. Here is a prayer you could use.

'Lord Jesus Christ, I admit that I have sinned and have gone my own way. I am willing to turn, with your help, from all that I know is wrong. I believe that you died for me to take away my sins; and I want you to be the Lord and Master of my life. And now I ask you to come in. Come into my life, Lord Jesus, to be my Saviour, my Friend and my Lord for ever. Thank you, Lord Jesus. Amen.'

Have you now prayed that? Well, believe that Jesus has *now answered your prayer* and has come into your life in the person of the Holy Spirit. As from now seek to live each day knowing that he is with you and will never leave you.

Jesus every day

That personal prayer, of course, was only a beginning: a vital, indispensable step, but much more is to follow, as with every true relationship. The Christian life is not a matter of rules and regulations, nor of feelings and experiences – primarily – but a steady, deepening relationship for the rest of one's life. When you meet someone for the first time it is unlikely that there will be a radical change in your life overnight. Normally the friendship must deepen, and that takes time. For further reading, see *New Life, New Lifestyle* by Michael Green (Hodder & Stoughton), an excellent book full of practical help.

It may be helpful thinking of three sets of relationships.

1 My relationship with God

The apostle Peter once wrote, 'You have been born anew, not of perishable seed but of imperishable, through the living and abiding word of God.... That word is the good news which was preached to you.' (1 Peter 1: 23, 25) When you invite Christ into your life, the Holy Spirit creates within you a spiritual birth. You are therefore 'born again,' born into God's family.

● 'How do I know that I am born again?' John answers that in his first letter. It is like sitting on a three-legged stool. If all three legs are there, you are in a stable position! If only two or one support you, there may be trouble! What are these 'legs?'

Firstly, the Word of God (1 John 5: 11–12). We must trust Christ's promises (e.g. Revelation 3: 20; John 6: 37; John 10: 28; Matthew 11: 28–30), being quietly confident that he really does mean what he says.

Secondly, the work of Christ (1 John 1: 7). All our sins, without exception, are washed clean by the blood of Jesus. Because of this, we can have absolute assurance of our relationship with God (see also Hebrews 10: 19–23).

Thirdly, the witness of the Spirit. John talks of many new developments in our life that can assure us of our new birth: a new desire to please God, a new love for God, a new hatred for sin, a new love for God's people, a new peace, a new power over temptation, a new reality in prayer ... (see 1 John 2: 3, 15, 29; 3: 9, 14, 21; 5: 4. 14). Like the blossom and fruit on a tree, these things will normally grow and develop slowly over a period of time. Together with these, there should be a deep inward assurance that God is our Father and we his children. (Romans 8: 15f)

● 'How can I grow in this new life?' Peter answers, 'Like newborn babes, long for the pure spiritual milk, that by it you may grow up to salvation; for you have tasted the kindness of the Lord.' (1 Peter 2: 2f)

As with every relationship we must spend time with Christ, primarily through personal Bible reading and prayer. Through the Bible Jesus can speak to us; through prayer we speak to him. Every day, if we possibly can, we need to find time, or *make* time (it is never easy), when we can be alone and quiet in his presence. Most Christians find that first thing in the morning, before the rush of the day has started, is the best time. For others, such as young mothers, that may be almost impossible. But we need to fight for these times when our relationship with Jesus can grow. There are various Bible reading methods such as those produced by Scripture Union, 130 City Road, London EC1V 2NJ, and it is wise to start with one of the Gospels, perhaps Mark or John. Many of the Psalms, too, are especially helpful (e.g. Psalms 1, 8, 23, 27, 32, 34, 40, 51, 84, 95, 96, 100, 103, 121, 139), and some of the shorter letters of the New Testament (e.g. Philippians, 1 Thessalonians, 1 Peter). Before you read, ask God to help you to understand the passage; the Bible is a spiritual book and we need the Holy Spirit to illuminate our minds with its truth. Moreover, we shall grasp God's truth insofar as we are willing to obey what is written.

Let God speak to you through the verses you are reading. Meditate on them or 'chew them over,' thinking quietly both about their meaning and about their special meaning for you. What is God saying here to *you*, in your situation today? Then talk back to God in prayer, using some of the thoughts from the Bible passage as the basis for your prayers. In this way a real two-way conversation between you and God can develop. There are, of course, many aspects of prayer. For further reading: *Pray in the Spirit* by Arthur Wallis (Kingsway), *Prayer* by O Hallesby (IVP), *Prayer Without Pretending* by Anne Townsend (SU). These aspects include:

Worship and praise, praising God for who he is and what he has done, both in creation and redemption. Many of the Psalms are helpful for this, and various New Testament passages such as Revelation 4 and 5.

Thanksgiving, thanking God for specific blessings or answers to prayer.

Confession, bringing before God anything on your conscience, being willing to turn right away from all that you know is wrong. Claim some promise of God's forgiveness such as 1 John 1 : 7, 9.

Intercession, praying for the needs of others and of yourself. Many find some simple prayer list or calendar of real help. You cannot pray for everyone every day! Therefore divide up the list of names and needs into different days of the week. Be business-like about prayer. All too often God has to say to us, 'You do not have what you want because you do not ask God for it.' (James 4: 2 (TEV))

Above all, ask God to fill you with his Holy Spirit. You have already received the Spirit into your life, if you have received Christ as your Lord and Saviour. But pray that your whole life might now be filled with, or controlled by, the Spirit. This was the vital power of the early Church, and of every Christian since then, whose life has really counted for God. It is the Spirit who will reveal Jesus and make God increasingly real in your experience. It is the Spirit who will help you to understand the Bible, lead you out in prayer, help you to praise and worship God, and fill your heart with his love. It is the Spirit who can give you the strength and power to live for Jesus every day, and to speak for Jesus as the opportunities arise. 'Be filled with the Spirit' is a command in the Scriptures (Ephesians 5:18), and the tense of the verb means 'go on being filled·with the Spirit day by day.' How?

In Luke 11:5–13 Jesus promised his disciples that his Father would certainly give the Spirit to those who ask him. The New Testament indicates that there are three important conditions which need to be fulfilled before this can happen. First, we must be willing to *repent* (Acts 2:38), or turn away, from any known sin, for the Spirit is the Holy Spirit and will not fill a vessel that wants to stay dirty. Second, we must be willing to *obey* (Acts 5:32) his leading in our lives; he wants to use us in God's service, not just to give us comforting or exciting spiritual experiences. Third, we must *hunger and thirst* (Matthew 5:6; John 7:37–39) for God's best for our lives; the Spirit wants to know that we really mean business. If those conditions are fulfilled, Jesus told us not to doubt, but to 'ask, and it will be given you; seek, and you will find; knock, and it will be opened to you.' And he told us not to be afraid, for 'what father among you, if his son asks for a fish, will instead of a fish give him a serpent; or if he asks for an egg, will give him a scorpion? If you then, who are evil know how to give good gifts to your children, how much more will the heavenly Father give the Holy Spirit to those who ask him!' (Luke 11:9, 11–13)

● 'What happens when I sin?' Sadly we all sin, many times. But the answer is positive and clear: 'If we confess our sins, (God) is faithful and just, and will forgive our sins and cleanse us from all unrighteousness.' (1 John 1:9) When we receive Jesus we begin both a new relationship and a new friendship. The new relationship is fixed: I can never cease to become the son of my heavenly Father. But the new friendship, like all friendships, is much more delicate. We shall need often to say sorry, to come back to Jesus, and to restore the friendship that we have damaged.

● 'Can I keep it up?' Answer: No, not in your own strength. But God 'is able to keep you from falling and to present you without blemish before the presence of his glory with rejoicing.' (Jude 24) When I walk down the road with my little son we often go hand-in-hand. Sometimes he stumbles on a stone, but I am holding his hand firmly and he does not fall. Frequently we stumble in our Christian walk with Jesus. But his promise is clear: 'They shall never perish, and no one shall snatch them out of my hand.' (John 10:28) By the strengthening power of the Spirit of Jesus within us, we are enabled to do what we could never do on our own.

Do not be surprised if at times you face real problems in your new-found faith, perhaps especially the temptation to doubt: doubting the reality of your faith or even of God himself. Indeed you should be surprised if problems do not arise! At the baptism of Jesus his Father assured him, 'You are my own dear Son....' Shortly afterwards Jesus, in the wilderness, was severely tempted by Satan: 'If you are God's Son.... If you are God's Son....' (Luke 3:22; 4:1–13 (TEV)) In the same way, you may face the same agonizing doubts shortly after you have received Jesus: 'If you are a Christian, why don't you feel different? If Jesus is with you, why does he seem so far away?' Three times Jesus countered Satan by quoting Scripture. Learn a few promises from God, and this can help enormously when faced with doubts.

Other problems, too, may upset you at times: absence of feeling, the apathy or scepticism of the world, getting nothing from prayer or from the Bible, being let down or disappointed by other Christians, puzzling questions you cannot answer, sudden tragedy or bereavement, failure and defeat, the old desires still very active for a way of life you know is wrong. Remember, however, that you have entered into a *relationship*, and all relationships have problems from time to time. For example, don't worry about those feelings. I am not sure that I 'feel' married at this moment (whatever that means) but I know that I am! Be open and honest with your problems. Talk to God about them, and, if possible, share them with an older, mature Christian friend. Paul once wrote: 'Every temptation that has come your way is the kind that normally comes to people. For God keeps his promise, and he will not allow you to be tempted beyond your power; but at the time you are tempted he will give you the strength to endure it, and so provide you with a way out.' (1 Corinthians 10: 13 (TEV))

2 My relationship with other Christians

Peter, using the building analogy says, 'Come to him (Jesus), to that living stone, rejected by men but in God's sight chosen and precious: and like living stones be yourselves built into a spiritual house....' (1 Peter 2: 4f)

If you saw some stones from a building lying in a heap on their own beside the building, it would be obvious that not only are they in the wrong place and useless, but the rest of the building would be considerably weakened by their absence. We, too, must be 'like living stones' firmly in place with the rest of the 'spiritual house.' We cannot go it alone. We need active fellowship with other Christians. And, should we mistakenly think that *we* do not need the help of others, they certainly need our help. John Wesley once said, 'Remember you cannot serve him alone; you must, therefore, find companions or make them; the Bible knows nothing of solitary religion.' The Christians in New Testament days come at once into fellowship with other disciples of Christ.

Therefore get involved with your local church or Christian Union or Christian fellowship (whatever it may be called). Go along to the services on Sunday and to meetings for Bible study and prayer. Get to know others who know and love Jesus. In some churches that may not be altogether easy. The apostle Paul had a very difficult time when he tried to join up with other Christians after his conversion. (Acts 9 : 26f) But he persevered because he knew it was important. Fellowship is one of God's ways of strengthening our faith; if we neglect this, we have only ourselves to blame for the problems that will certainly arise.

Of course, there are churches and churches! To begin with, at least, do your utmost to find one that is alive, that will give you good Bible teaching, that will help you to worship God and serve him. Link up with a small Bible study group as well, if you can, and welcome the help of a mature Christian for further guidance. With the right person this can be of the greatest help, as I found for the first few months of my Christian life. The more we get involved in Christian fellowship and service, the more the reality of Christ's presence will be experienced in our lives: 'Where two or three are gathered in my name, there am I in the midst of them.' (Matthew 18 : 20).

3 My relationship with the world

'You are ... a holy nation,' wrote Peter, 'God's own people, that you may declare the wonderful deeds of him who called you out of darkness into his marvellous light.' (1 Peter 2 : 9) Two facts emerge from this statement.

First, as God's own people, we are called to be 'holy.' There is nothing negative or killjoy about holiness. Its root meaning is to be 'set apart': set apart, that is, from sin to God. We need to *show* others by our lives that God is real, that Jesus is alive, and that his Spirit can make, indeed has made, all these things true. Nothing is more important than the unconscious influence of a life impregnated with the Spirit of Jesus. A major reason for Christ's own magnetic attraction was that he manifestly loved everyone, however 'worldly' or 'sinful' they might have been, and yet he himself was utterly different. Therefore they were puzzled and intrigued. Nothing is so powerful as a Christ-like life.

If we see ourselves as now set apart for Jesus, we must be careful about what we say and do. In practice, these three questions will nearly always guide you when you are not sure about a course of action:

● Will it help or hinder my Christian life? (Hebrews 12:1f)

● Will it help or hinder someone else's Christian life? (1 Corinthians 8:9ff)

● Is it to the glory of God? (1 Corinthians 10:31–11:1)

Or, summarizing these with one simple, searching test: Can I really pray about it? These are some of the questions that we must ask carefully and honestly before God, all the time letting God's word in the Bible be our guide concerning our life and behaviour.

Second, as God's own people, we are to *declare* his wonderful deeds, or to be witnesses to Jesus. The Christian faith is to be shared. God loves the whole world. Christ has died 'for our sins, and not for ours only but also for the sins of the whole world.' (1 John 2:2) It is a part of a Christian's responsibility and privilege to help others find Christ too. Your immediate responsibility is your own circle of friends and acquaintances. If you are not an effective 'missionary' – and a missionary is simply someone 'sent by God' – in that circle there is no other Christian in the world who can do that work for you. Learn as much as you can about the Christian faith, discovering how to answer some of the questions that are raised time and time again. Be very clear, especially, as to how you could guide another person in his search for God. A simple framework might be as follows:

● A Something to *Admit*   The fact of sin and the need for forgiveness: Romans 3: 23; 6: 23; Isaiah 59: 2

● B Something to *Believe*   Christ has died to take away your sin: Isaiah 53: 5–6; 1 Peter 2: 24; 3: 18

● C Something to *Consider*   Christ must come first in your life: Mark 8: 34–38

● D Something to *Do*   Ask Christ into your life: Revelation 3: 20

Many are confused about the reality of God or their personal relationship with him. Therefore a logical sequence of steps, with verses, can be of the greatest help. However, we must never throw texts at people; but rather, with the sensitivity of love, seek to show them the truth about Jesus in whatever way we can. Above all, pray for the Spirit's guidance, remembering that God is searching for us long before we begin to search for him.